VAN HALEN

The Reverb series looks at the connections between music, artists and performers, musical cultures and places. It explores how our cultural and historical understanding of times and places may help us to appreciate a wide variety of music, and vice versa.

reverb-series.co.uk
Series editor: John Scanlan

Already published

The Beatles in Hamburg
Ian Inglis

VAN HALEN

EXUBERANT CALIFORNIA, ZEN ROCK'N'ROLL

JOHN SCANLAN

REAKTION BOOKS

Published by Reaktion Books Ltd
33 Great Sutton Street
London ECIV ODX, UK
www.reaktionbooks.co.uk

First published 2012

Printed and bound in Great Britain
by Bell & Bain, Glasgow

British Library Cataloguing in Publication Data
    Scanlan, John, 1964–
    Van Halen : exuberant California, Zen rock'n'roll. – (Reverb)
    1. Van Halen (Musical group) 2. Rock music – California – 1971–1980.
    I. Title II. Series
    782.4'2166'0922-DC23

ISBN 9 781 86189 916 3

CONTENTS

PREFACE 7

1 OUT UPON THE OCEAN 11

2 ISLANDS: SUNSET STRIP AND THE 1970s, *c.* 1974–7 21

3 THE GOLDEN DREAM, CALIFORNIA 49

4 HANGING TEN, *c.* 1977–82 67

5 HOLLYWOOD FLOTSAM, *c.* 1980–82 87

6 THE TAO OF DAVE: SURF LIFE 101

7 DIVER DOWN, TEMPERATURE UP, *c.* 1981–2 120

8 THINK LIKE THE WAVES, LIKE A CHILD, *c.* 1982–3 133

9 SAIL TO THE MOON 155

10 WIPEOUT, *c.* 1984–2007 175

Chronology 189
References 193
Discography and Soundtrack 207
Photo Acknowledgements 208
Index 209

PREFACE

Van Halen, a critic once noted, seemed to have developed a style that was 'halfway between a Los Angeles traffic jam and an abstract painting'.[1] It was an observation that sensed that, whatever it was that they were doing, they were just making it – this rock'n'roll – up as they went along.

Formed in 1973, Van Halen seemed to plough through every bar, high school gym, bowling alley and dance club in the Los Angeles area until, in 1978, they arrived to the wider world in a style that seemed to live up to the spirit of youthful exuberance that so marked the culture of Southern California, if not to a passion for rock'n'roll as the unregulated expenditure of energy. Free-falling from the skies above Anaheim Stadium they arrived onstage with air-raid sirens blaring as they pulled off parachutes and flying helmets.

Or that was how it looked, anyway.

It emerged sometime later that it had all, in fact, been an elaborate hoax. The band members hid in a trailer as the real skydivers hit the ground behind the stage, ready to leap out on cue. As Van Halen – third on the bill – ran out to gasps from an incredulous audience it seemed that they had achieved the desired aim that day which, as singer David Lee Roth later said, was to see what '62,000 people fainting at once' might have looked like; and 'to prove that Van Halen were not earthbound'.[2] In that, they fell into sync with a loose set of ideals that Kevin Starr has described as characteristic of 'Zen California'. Zen California was a state of mind, an idea of a time and place, and of a way of being that celebrated 'the now'; that rode on its passion for the moment in a manner that could be seen elsewhere in much Southern Californian culture. It was present, most obviously, in the practice of surfing – the pre-eminent Californian art of mind, body and nature that was defined by a receptivity to the moment.[3]

For Van Halen, rock'n'roll would release them from the claim of time and the gravity of work, and put them into play just as the waves played the surfers. Thus, Eddie Van Halen, guitarist extraordinaire, claimed his ambition was not just to be a musician and a writer of songs, but also to 'fall off the edge of buildings'. On his side was David Lee Roth, the singer who sailed onstage like some kind of mutant latter-day samurai – sometimes stumbling like a drunk, occasionally moving like a ballet dancer or a circus acrobat, or 'hanging ten' on the sonic waves as he sang on 1978's 'On Fire'. (To 'hang ten' is to balance on the tip of the surfboard with one's toes on the edge, a manoeuvre that is thought to demonstrate the unity of mind, body and environment in 'the moment'.)

What motivated this passion to be loosened from the kind of constraints that kills the spirit of youth was a belief in a certain idea of rock'n'roll. It was a Zen-like idea in that it was attached to the creative unconscious in a way that flew against rock music's growing seriousness in the 1970s. In singer Roth's case the unconscious was the 'no-mind' of Zen, which advocated a childlikeness that he articulated and, in many ways, personified. For Eddie Van Halen the unconscious was encountered in a manner more common to aesthetic romanticism, and to the synaesthetic dimensions of sound, music and feeling. Thus his music, he once said enigmatically, was above all else 'brown'. Along with drummer Alex Van Halen and bassist Michael Anthony they produced what might be thought of as a kind of California Zen rock'n'roll.

This book looks at Van Halen's emergence in the Hollywood of the early to mid-1970s and their relation to a California both real and idealized, which, the reader will see, makes it almost inconceivable to think of them as emerging from another time and place. It situates the sustained creative period of their rise to prominence amid the culture of Los Angeles – the pre-eminent city of popular music – their residencies in the legendary clubs of the Sunset Strip, the studios where they made their albums and their relationship to a series of passing musical trends, including the glam, punk and alternative scenes of the 1970s and early 1980s. Underlying it all, though, is an exploration of the people who existed at the centre of a surge of creative energy that would produce a series of best-selling albums between 1978 and 1984, and see Van Halen – for a moment in 1983 – become the highest-earning performers in concert history.

That distinction, however, marked the beginning of the end of the relationship of the band's two most prominent figures, Eddie Van Halen and David Lee Roth, which was wiped out just as the band finally conquered the charts and went global.

Van Halen: Exuberant California, Zen Rock'n'roll concludes with an account of what became of Van Halen in the aftermath of those decades when the waning of youthful exuberance seemed to dilute the spirit of the rock'n'roll that had made them so characteristically Californian, and so in tune with Zen California.

Van Halen onstage, Miami, Florida, 1982. David Lee Roth (bareback, at centre of shot) would remark: 'People say we don't take this stuff seriously – I say you don't stand on a boat with stiff legs.' In the foreground, sporting a convict outfit, is Alex Van Halen.

1 OUT UPON THE OCEAN

Reality – every kind of reality – may be perceived as a particular deployment or arrangement of things to be relied upon
and worked to one's advantage.

– François Jullien, *The Propensity of Things*

Asked in 1980 if he might consider himself to be trash culture's
greatest ever product, Van Halen's David Lee Roth gave an unusual
answer. Rather than being insulted by the suggestion that he might
be no more than the latest passing fad, ripe for disposal, he was
rather engaged with what it might mean to be trash. 'I don't know
if I'm the ultimate product', he replied. 'What is "ultimate trash"?
God, maybe I could ascend to that.' He thought for a while, and
realized that, of course, it had to be. 'Yeah, yeah!' he said. 'Definitely.'[1]

Trash is, if nothing else, a two-faced thing – once the stuff of
desire, it becomes, by and by, relegated to a kind of nothingness.
It speaks, perhaps, of the lures and traps of desire itself, which
may promise happiness but, in fact, only reveals the truth of its
transience. Trash is what it is because it slips out of our grasp.
To aspire to such a condition – a thought that tickled the Zen-
minded Roth – is, when all is said and done, to be at one with the
impermanence of existence itself. Most of us battle against this;
against giving ourselves up to the world, but for the Taoist such
an aspiration makes perfect sense.

The temperamental counterpart of trash's transience and
negation of the desire *to be* is stupidity; a mute absence and denial
of 'self' that points to the horror of a meaningless existential void.
As Roth once said – and not without coincidence – 'for many
people, Van Halen represent the abyss'. Or, as Charles M. Young
of *Musician* magazine once put it in 1984, the band Roth fronted

presented a conundrum to anyone who might want to fix it with a label. Who were they? What were they? 'Van Halen' were, he suggested:

(a) The Four Stooges, (b) more murderous than Abdullah the Butcher [the wrestler], (c) what would happen if you put Al Jolson in the studio with Beethoven, (d) lucky it hasn't run into a bridge abutment, (e) the best, (f) all of the above.[2]

When he first met Roth in 1984, Young figured that what he was facing was clearly a manifestation of the mythical figure of the trickster – he who collapses the boundaries of all thought and action that enable us to neatly organize the world.[3] This was why the closer Young looked – he had predicted in a review of *Van Halen* for *Rolling Stone* magazine in 1978 that they would be a bloated FM rock band within a few years – the less easy it was to grasp what was there. As the American mythographer Joseph Campbell wrote, the trickster 'always breaks in, just as the unconscious does, to trip up the rational situation. He's both a fool and someone who's beyond the system.'[4] In myth, he is manifested in the form of innumerable slippery, elusive figures: Hermes, Reynard the Fox, Brer Rabbit and countless others. In popular culture he is Batman's Joker, Robin Hood, the cartoon Wiley E. Coyote or Clint Eastwood in the guise of 'The Man With No Name', whose trickery Roth borrowed in Van Halen's 'Hang 'em High'. As he told *Spin* magazine in 1986:

The man who came from nowhere and goes home to no one. I always felt that. I always had a real good time with it . . . I'm living it. I'm breathing it.[5]

As Lewis Hyde notes in *Trickster Makes This World*, 'all tricksters are "on the road".' They represent 'the spirit of the doorway leading out, and of the crossroad at the edge of town'.[6] Of all the members of Van Halen, it is perhaps not surprising that Roth was the one who never settled down or got married; the one who harboured a romantic ideal about being on the road – whether that meant being in a rock'n'roll band, or adventuring in the Himalayas (he conquered κ2, the world's second-highest peak, and only failed to surmount Everest due to bad weather) or getting lost in some remote jungle (as he did in Amazonia, in 1983). And like the trickster figure, whose chief aim was to sow the seeds of confusion, and to buck the rules of the system – to reveal their true workings – Roth, too, was really up to no good. He was deceitful and shameless, 'amoral', Young noted, 'driven by appetites' rather than reason or logic, and getting away with stuff in a way that no one else could – *and* doing it with a childlike glee.[7] 'If you're getting a bad impression of me', he would tell journalists, 'spread it around.'

Van Halen's rise to the top of the US charts coincided with the era during which various rock'n'roll baddies were the target of a holy alliance of conservative interests; self-appointed guardians of cultural standards who spent too much time spinning vinyl records backwards in search of 'satanic' messages. In Roth's lyrical imagery, though, they would have found nothing more disturbing than allusions to Max Fleischer's odd, spooky cartoon from the 1930s, *Swing You Sinners!* Nevertheless, when the so-called Washington Wives, led by Tipper Gore (wife of later vice-president, Al Gore) were campaigning against the perceived evils of popular music and for the values of what they termed the 'moral majority', Roth was quick to declare himself toastmaster general of the *immoral* majority, just as others who took all this seriously queued up to deny the accusations in front of Congressional hearings. When Roth declared to journalists that he wouldn't 'go down in history, but I [would] go down on your sister', you were never quite sure if he really meant it, or if he was just – like the trickster – collapsing the boundaries of thought and action, saying exactly what should not be said in public. Perhaps he, and Van Halen, were channelling the Three Stooges, acting as irritants to respectability.

In fact, Roth's behaviour provoked the kind of response that lived up to the central ambiguity of a trickster figure. That is to say, he divided opinion – even among self-declared Van Halen fans. In this, he led Van Halen with him to some extent, but more often stood out as the main offender against good taste. As rock'n'roll outfits go, this was a band of formidable musical ability – a band able to make their musical peers 'sound like sluggish, unimagina-tive hacks', as the *Los Angeles Times* noted in 1982. Yet, here they were – in the public imagination at least – 'powered by love-him-or-loathe him vocalist David Lee Roth' and his 'narcissistic swag-ger'.[8] As Henry Rollins (the frontman of Los Angeles punks Black Flag) recalled:

> People I knew who didn't usually voice their opinions,
> always had an opinion about that guy. Either they were into
> Dave or they wanted to punch that grin right off his face.[9]

Rollins was one of Roth's fans, but nonetheless felt able to say that he 'could see why a lot of people hated his guts'.[10] How could Roth, on the one hand, be capable of executing those quasi-balletic, martial arts moves that saw him spend much of his time during live shows off the ground and sailing through the air, yet on the other, be a fall-down drunk; a man running off too much junk food and sugar, to say nothing of more illicit substances?

Roth's ability to make even his own audience uncomfortable did not diminish with the passing of the years, with one witness to his ill-fated mid-1990s stint in Las Vegas suggesting that his 'penchant for rambling fictional scenarios, extended blues jams and oblique Zen humor . . . tests the attention span' of even his most loyal fans:

> More than any other rock act or Vegas veteran, Roth
> reminds one of Sandra Bernhard in his ability to dispense
> comedy, discomfort, *pensées* and musical homages in one
> unwholesome package.[11]

This was the kind of response that was common among critics,
who seemed to be both repulsed by Roth yet drawn unaccountably
to him, and thus to Van Halen. The following reaction – the
opening salvo from an article in *Rolling Stone* in 1979 – was fairly
typical of the need many writers felt, if they were going to say
anything positive about the band, to first outline some of the
problems they had with the mere idea and presence of them:

> Van Halen is the latest rock act to fall out of a family tree
> of deadbeats whose ancestry includes slave drummers on
> Roman galleys, Ginger Baker's Air Force and the street
> crews of the New York City Department of Sanitation.[12]

The article's author, Timothy White, nonetheless ended by saying
that, in the *Van Halen II* album (the subject of his article) this
'blockbusting four-man outfit' had created an 'amazing' artefact
that might astound distant generations of rock archaeologists.
For the most part, however, it was Roth's lack of self-discipline
and modesty that had critics reaching for their notebooks. *There'll
always be people in the peanut gallery throwing stuff at you* was the
kind of thing he might utter in response, therein painting a picture
of the critics as noisy upstarts in the 'cheap seats', not unlike the
hard-to-please children of the TV show *Howdy Doody* (1950s), who
delivered instantaneous judgements on the entertainment from
their own little peanut gallery.

    Cynthia Rose, writing about Van Halen's *Diver Down* album
of 1982 for the *New Musical Express* (*NME*), heaped praise on the
musicality of the band, particularly brothers Eddie and Alex Van

Halen, but observed that, while 'the tunes more than pass muster
. . . no quarter is given for anyone to *get used* to front man David
Lee Roth'.[13] With the benefit of hindsight, this reaction was merely
a further development in Rose's seeming inability to rid herself
of the spectre of the so-called 'Diamond Dave' and Van Halen.
In truth she seemed destined always to be the one who would try
to answer the question that Charles Young of *Musician* would pose
– what, or who, is Van Halen? In *NME* – not entirely known for its
support for long-haired American rockers – she always ended up
with the job of reviewing the band's new albums; and, while she
could never really hide the fact that there was some fascination
there, that maybe she really liked them a great deal, it was an
acceptance that was always equally cut through with disgust.
She had been conned by these tricksters into liking this 'thing'.
In her review of *Fair Warning* (1981), for instance, Rose was – as
on other occasions – impressed with what the band had served
up, musically. 'These guys do architect actual and varied songs',
she said, 'from *Fair Warning*'s stinging "Sinners Swing!" and vivid
"Mean Streets" to the hyperkinetic "Unchained" . . .'

> this LP's best numbers are constructed around Eddie's
> whip-you-with-electric-eels showmanship and buoyed up
> by brother Alex's Oblique Strategies drumming – which
> lashes the cymbals, varies the support system and attacks
> from behind instead of coming down on top of the rhythm
> in traditional thump and grind fashion.[14]

Yet, once again when it came to 'love-him-or-loathe him' singer
Roth, she felt compelled to lay at his door not only the blame
for 'the sheer unbelievable obnoxiousness of the band's sartorial
gambits' – she did have a point in that regard – but personal
responsibility for 'Van Halen's successful vandalism of Western
rock's disarray'.[15] Roth, however, slipping free of the grasp of the

critic, was already one step ahead and turned those kinds of observations back at their source. 'Sure, Van Halen is storm and thunder', he told Don Waller in the *Los Angeles Times*:

> *Sturm und Drang*, delivered at high velocity and close intervals. It's preposterous in magnitude. It's all bluster – a big fireball that eats itself up. You've gotta laugh at that sometimes. Look at the *clothes* I wear [Laughs *real* hard].[16]

It was almost as though he was saying – 'anything bad you say about me and my band, I can outdo; you can't even beat me when it comes to criticizing myself.' But by 1984 you could have been forgiven for thinking she had always been a fan, as she congratulated Roth for reaching a level of 'career construction that outstrips even that of Bob Dylan'.[17] Who knows what that meant, but it was a kind of accommodation – a throwing up of the hands to say: 'Okay! I give in. You win.' Perhaps she saw that Roth, like Dylan, was a shape-shifter who fled any attempt to pin him down: a slippery fellow who had now earned the right to get away with it, or to get some recognition for remaining true to his tricksy ways. Indeed this might explain her appraisal of Van Halen's *MCMLXXXIV / 1984* album, captured in a piece of writing which itself took the form of an elaborate ruse any trickster would have been proud of. Within a summary of the album's supposed influences comes the following:

> The literary sources behind this album are two minor classics of the late 1930s: Leemings' *Fun with String* (Pub. Frederick A. Stokes) and *Betcha Can't Do It* ('how to put 12 persons in 11 beds and other intriguing stunts guaranteed to break the ice at any party') by Alex van Rensselaer, publisher Appleton-Century. Don't be deceived by the small 'v' in van Rensselaer. The two Van Halens are almost certainly distant blood

relations of some sort, for *much* ideological pilfering from the obscure but original manual has taken place on numbers such as 'Panama', 'Girl Gone Bad', and 'Top Jimmy'.[18]

This fiction caught the spirit of Roth and Van Halen as accurately as anyone had, and also inadvertently threw light on something else without perhaps being entirely aware of it – the absent artistic 'I' of Roth, which flew in the face of the fetishism of authenticity, which so defined rock music and the most thoughtless and unimaginative examples of its associated criticism.

Elsewhere, the 'love-them-and-loathe-them' reaction to Van Halen was equally in evidence. Barney Hoskyns could say in one breath that while 'David Lee Roth is clearly a disgusting Hollywood pig', Van Halen were, for all their 'meaningless flashiness' what he 'loved about rock'n'roll in the first place'. The point was not just that Van Halen had good tunes, but that they were 'human, with funk and feel to spare'.[19]

All such signs of revulsion, grudging approval and, indeed, love and enthusiasm for Roth can perhaps be related back to this idea of the trickster; to a sense of being manipulated by someone by their playing around with you. For the critics, it might have seemed that they were there for Roth's entertainment, and not the other way around; or, as Alex Van Halen once put it, 'We see ourselves as social workers – our job is to keep rock critics in work.' 'We *love* to read the reviews', Roth said in 1980. 'The worse they hate us, the more colourful the adjectives they have to use, the more scenes they have to paint to explain *why*. It makes great reading.'[20] As Lewis Hyde notes, those who come to be described by the term 'trickster' get to have it both ways; they are, indeed, 'the lords of in-between'. The trickster is 'the creative idiot . . . the wise fool, the grey-haired baby, the cross-dresser, the speaker of profanities'.[21]

Who or what, then, were Van Halen? For *Creem* magazine's Dave DiMartino, lambasted by his colleagues for confessing that

he 'loved and was captivated by Van Halen' in a well-known profile of the band, 'they existed in an interesting place . . . a sort of
pre-post ironic age. They were really good at acting like morons
and knowing they were acting like morons.'[22]

In fact, they embodied a spirit and attitude that – as we will
see – makes them uniquely Californian. Emerging in the 'loose'
and less uptight early 1970s, they felt compelled to live in the
moment, to glorify play over work, to celebrate the power of
a childlike unconscious and to revel in the accidental nature
of who they were and what they became. They were vulgar
– but no less than California had itself always been deemed
the land of the vulgar, and the capital of trash culture. And like
California, they seemed to exist in such a way – eyes set on the
immediate, moving at a pace that seemed unsustainable – that
willed its own destruction. But that, too, was very rock'n'roll.

The 'do not care' attitude of rock'n'roll, of course, is ambig-
uous and non-committal – an expression of cool detachment –
but rock'n'roll is also about *not* holding any energy in reserve.
It is, in its essence, an expression of pure exuberance. Thus Van
Halen's music was meant to 'explode', they said; it produced
eruptions, aimed to live its life like there was no tomorrow. As
Roth said, what they were about was energy and enthusiasm; they
were a big fireball that could do no more than consume itself. Van
Halen's exuberance produced a kind of 'unthinking', unassuming
– but often exhilarating – rock'n'roll that was evocative of its time
and place. But, like much of Californian culture, it was touched by
a Zen-like attitude to everyday life. Like the Beat poets and writers
who tried to live out their art in accordance with Zen ideals, going
with the flow – or, more accurately perhaps, being part of a wave
that they did not seek to control or direct – was Van Halen's guiding idea. They might have been, in that respect, some kind of weird
Pop Art experiment in which the *idea* almost determined the thing
itself; which underlined – in process and reception, that is to say –

the object that was the result of the creative effort. Perhaps that's why Roth could tell a journalist in 1980 that their new stage show would be 'a hodgepodge, just like my apartment. We'll just throw some stuff in and see where it lands.'[23] And that, in fact, is just what it felt and sounded like as it unfolded, as one journalist noted in terms commonly used by parents everywhere:

> Untidy. Muddled. Dishevelled. Disorganised . . . Like a collection of kids tiring of their presents on Christmas Day, the attention spans of the various Van Halen band members seemed limited. Almost as soon as they started a number, they became bored with it.[24]

Well, for Van Halen, Alice Cooper's most famous declaration rang more true than it would for most: school *was* out – and out forever. Their motivation, however, also has to be understood within the context of what historian Kevin Starr has termed 'Zen California' – a state of mind that occupies the temporality of play, and lives out the ideals of eternal youth.[25] 'Childlikeness has to be restored', wrote Daisetz Suzuki, the thinker who popularized a peculiarly American variant of Zen that seemed to mesh perfectly with Californian culture. It was necessary to train oneself in 'the art of self forgetfulness':

> When this is attained, man thinks yet he does not think. He thinks like the showers coming down from the sky; he thinks like the waves rolling on the ocean . . . indeed, he is the showers, the ocean.[26]

The essence of play and the route to creativity, as the work of Van Halen seemed to suggest, was indeed to be found in forgetting oneself; in doing without thinking, and in disregarding the strictures of the adult world of responsibility – in living in the now.

2 ISLANDS: SUNSET STRIP AND THE 1
c. 1974–7

> People assume we're a Hollywood band, but Hollywood's like
> New York. There are islands.
>
> – Eddie Van Halen, 1979

For a few years in the mid- to late 1960s the 1.7-mile section of
Sunset Boulevard in West Hollywood known as the 'Strip' was
home to a music scene that, for a time, displaced the adjacent
movie studios as the hub of cultural activity on the West Coast.
In the decades before the 1960s it had been home to a thriving
nightlife, which contained no shortage of the kind of excess and
decadence seen in later decades. But, as Barney Hoskyns has
written, that was all crucially before 'the dawn of Teenage'.[1] It
was teen culture that effected the most radical change to Sunset
Strip – to this part of Hollywood – making it a bellwether for
gauging the movements of a new and less deferential ethos, a
different sense of this time and place that held out the possibility
of creating a new culture. As Domenic Priore wrote:

> The fruits of LA's teen megalopolis, and the remnants it
> left behind transformed the mid 1960s Sunset Strip into a
> fascinating artistic Mecca . . . teens could interact freely
> and creatively with budding youth icons in clubs that had
> previously been the exclusive domain of the rich and famous
> of the 1930s and 1940s.[2]

The youth icons in question were none other than the members
of the pop bands that had rapidly appeared following The Beatles'
storming of America in 1964. But what was taking place in the

1960s represented something more than the appearance of a
new generation of night creatures – they appeared to be of
a different kind than the Strip's older denizens. Showing more
self-consciousness than any previous generation had, the young
people sought to separate themselves from the values of older
generations. In this, they would be fuelled by the twin highs of
popular music and drugs.

The new music of the Sunset Strip – made by bands such as
The Doors, Love, Buffalo Springfield and The Byrds – developed
a distinctive Californian flavour cooked up from ingredients that
elsewhere might not have come together. Could The Byrds' 'Mr
Tambourine Man', with the languorous morning haze of its
opening notes, have existed without the soothing warmth of the
sun? Was it possible to hear The Doors' dreamlike 'Moonlight
Drive' without believing that the Pacific Ocean possessed powers
of seduction? This sense of popular music being more readily in
tune with the sensibilities of place would provide the first evidence
that the capital of rock'n'roll had shifted from its most recent
epicentre in London to Los Angeles. In the streets of Hollywood
and amid the hills that snaked off to the north of Sunset Boulevard – if not in Los Angeles more generally – the music of the
time also came to be inseparable from a number of soon-to-be
legendary recording studios that just happened to be in the
neighbourhood. It was as if the whole of the West Coast music
industry was contained in its own little village; which, in a way,
was close to the truth.

In Western Recorders, Sunset Sound Recorders, the Village
Recorders and other studios, many of the most seminal recordings
in popular music in that or any other era were made. Everyone
from Angeleno natives such as Phil Spector, Eddie Cochran,
Ritchie Valens and The Beach Boys to British bands like The
Rolling Stones and Led Zeppelin would work in these studios
on some of their most durable music. This Los Angeles – this

Hollywood – represented, as Drew Tewksbury notes, an alternative
studio city to that of movieland. And at the time it matched, in its
influence and reach, the film studios of Los Angeles that we more
readily associate with the name Hollywood.[3]

This period's impact on those who lived through it – which
would ultimately be transmitted to the wider world, thanks to its
music – was found locally in places like Venice Beach and obviously
the Sunset Strip itself. There, Eric Avila notes, 'the children of
Southern California's great white middle class reveled in an alternative set of sensations and experiences', not the least of which
included 'smoking marijuana, dropping acid, and drowning in
the rebellious sounds' of this new music scene.[4]

Yet the emergence of this new kind of culture was not immedi-
ately to everyone's liking, and it is easy to forget how little out of
its infancy the phenomenon of rock'n'roll was, and the extent to
which what happened in the early to mid-1960s was almost the
second wind of a culture that seemed to have blown itself out at
the close of the 1950s. As Domenic Priore flatly notes, it was no
surprise that 'many people in mid-60s LA hated rock and roll'.
They took their antipathy to what was happening on the street –
among young people, in particular – as the basis for what has since
been described as one of the last significant cultural wars to take
place in the USA, over who had the right to this few square miles of
land.[5] Those who hated rock'n'roll were the usual suspects – busi-
nessmen, local politicians and the Los Angeles Police Department.
They 'longed to see it eradicated' and the Strip purged of the
swarming crowds of longhairs who had suddenly appeared as
if from nowhere, like aliens from an unwelcome future that lay
ominously on the horizon.[6] The result of this clash of cultures
was that, by 1966, police harassment of teenagers on Sunset Strip
became increasingly routine and indiscriminate. It supplied the
visual imagery for Buffalo Springfield's Top 10 hit of January 1967,
'For What It's Worth', the epitome of mid-1960s youthful alienation,

which spoke more broadly to the disengagement of young people from the kind of authority that had sanctioned the war in Vietnam. Its evocation of a paranoia born in the long shadows of baton-wielding cops – 'There's a man with a truncheon over there / Telling me, I got to beware' – was glimpsed as the dying light of Sunset Strip's once radiant youth culture.

The ensuing street confrontations between the forces of the old and new cultures even inspired a cash-in movie, *Riot on Sunset Strip* (dir. Arthur Dreifuss, 1967), featuring a song of the same name by The Standells) that took the side of those who wanted the place cleaned up. The real riots were followed eventually by curfews and an attempt to shut down the busy club scene.

What ultimately lay beneath the hostility of the Los Angeles establishment to life on the Strip was, of course, money. The prize at stake, in particular, would be the riches to be found in long-cherished property deals, as the Strip was imagined into the form of a number of plots, just waiting to be sold off or carved up for further profits. But while the Strip escaped such radical dreams of redevelopment, what it suffered in the aftermath of the riots was the loss of many of the venues that had, earlier in the decade, made it precisely more like the centre of a social revolution than simply some kind of open air entertainment complex. The show-down on Sunset Strip in 1966 thus brought to an end a particular phase of Southern California's musical culture.

At the end of the 1960s the Strip had fewer venues and a less visible night life – its relative decline was mirrored in the fact that most of the bands associated with it had, more or less, fled together to nearby rural retreats like Laurel Canyon, set in the Hollywood Hills behind the Strip.[7]

Van Halen first reached the Strip some seven years after all this, in early 1974 (although it seems that the Van Halen brothers had failed a number of club auditions on the Strip earlier in the decade,

Police on Sunset Boulevard corral crowds during the riots of 1966. Within little more than a year the Strip's nightlife had been all but closed down, and would only witness crowds like this some ten years later.

possibly in 1971–2). It was in Hollywood that they would spend most of the next four years. And, like The Doors before them, and Guns N' Roses in the 1980s, they became for a time the 'house band' at Gazzarri's – which, signalling the audience it appealed to, was offering cash prizes to the best dancers in the audience. The venue had survived the period of the riots and their aftermath – where others had hit the wall – due to some skilful manoeuvring on the part of the owner, Bill Gazzarri, which had ensured that he was not stripped of his entertainment licence.[8] Many other clubs weren't so fortunate. The Strip may have been the hub of the Los Angeles music scene (and popular music more widely) just a few short years before, but by the early 1970s it was beginning to take on a more ghostly appearance as young Angelinos seemed to abandon the streets. Elmer Valentine – the owner of the Whisky A Go Go – told the *Los Angeles Herald Examiner* that the purging of so-called undesirable elements from the Strip had left the place feeling somewhat deserted. So much so, that it would be quite feasible, he said, to blast 'a cannon down the middle of Sunset Boulevard and not worry about hitting anyone'.[9]

The sense of decline was matched in American society more generally, with the years 1973–4 inaugurating a number of significant changes that affected the social and cultural climate of that strange decade. The US withdrawal from Vietnam in 1973, which represented a significant failure, was soon followed by the resignation of the disgraced President Nixon in 1974 and the beginning of the Middle East oil embargo, which raised prices and saw long queues at gas stations (it also led to vinyl shortages that affected the music industry). This was also the beginning of a recession that would last most of the rest of the decade.[10] And in 1974, too, an observer attuned to the more widespread sense of social and cultural malaise would not have failed to gasp in wonder at the irony of the iconic Hollywood sign – perhaps the ultimate Californian icon – crumbling to pieces as a result of neglect, as if the abandonment of the Strip had spread into the hills, turning once solid structures to ruins. Like the economy, the Hollywood sign remained in a bad state until near the end of the decade – until 1978, when some public-minded celebrities raised a campaign to save it from total collapse (Alice Cooper, a patron of the Strip's bars and clubs during the 1970s, donated $28,000 to save the letter 'O'). The eclipse of the optimistic 1960s was, in other words, all around; it was in the air, and it manifested itself in a feeling that everything had stopped. As Van Halen's David Lee Roth later noted in his autobiography, the 1970s were like one long 'time out'.

This 'time out' – or half time – manifested itself in myriad ways. As Sam Binkley has argued, while the 1960s are seen as an era of liberation, it was really in the 1970s that the earlier decade's consequences were played out and carried into wider cultural changes. Young (*and* older) people who lived through the 1970s became even more relaxed, *looser* and less inhibited than at any time before: 'The loose life dwelled in the textures of daily life and the minutiae of personal experience . . .'

> It was lived in the immediacy of *the now* – a real life one could really experience. To 'be yourself', to 'do what was right for you', to 'let it all hang out' was to release a primordial vitality, to become an artist of oneself.[11]

This roughly drawn individualism was seen also to mark the Los Angeles music scene of the 1970s, which had also quickly turned into a different kind of entity. By contrast with the sense of youthful togetherness that many felt had characterized the Strip in the mid-1960s, the atmosphere in the following decade – the 'me decade' as Tom Wolfe said – is most often described in terms of a kind of cocaine-fuelled elitism. This was particularly evident at clubs such as The Troubadour and the Roxy, where the new kings and queens of the country rock that had come to dominate the LA music industry since the late 1960s, held court.[12] 'For LA's budding rock royalty', Michael Walker notes,

> coke was conspicuous consumption as an exercise in meticulous countercultural circumspection, a choice safely within bounds but still a status marker among one's fellow millionaire singer-songwriters.[13]

That there were now multimillionaires among those budding youth icons of a few years previously reveals the extent to which the music industry had succeeded in transforming the scene into product. In marked contrast to the Hollywood of the mid-1960s, this new 'rock royalty' kept some distance from whatever remnants of the Strip's teen culture had persisted. Unsurprisingly, this included whatever was happening at Gazzarri's, where the unknown, the unhip and the overlooked – including Van Halen – found themselves hosting dance nights for, as Roth often said, doughnut waitresses from Canoga Park.

Although separated by only a few years in terms of age, the gulf between the unknown Van Halen and the more established bands of the day, who either lived or entertained themselves in Hollywood, is perhaps illustrated by an encounter that took place one night in 1975 at the Rainbow Bar and Grill. The now legendary bar – wedged between The Roxy and Gazzarri's – had, as Michael Walker notes, 'the feel of a pirate's ship run aground in the middle of the Strip'.[14] It was a watering hole beloved of British musicians and their hangers-on, who would spend a lot of time in Hollywood – they liked it partly because they felt relatively safe from the unwanted attention of fans but were, importantly, still accessible to the numerous willing groupies. This was all due to the care the club's doormen took over them. One night, though, Eddie and Alex Van Halen stopped in between sets at Gazzarri's and approached the table of Led Zeppelin's John Bonham, introducing themselves as members of a band playing a mere stone's throw away. The burly drummer – later known to have a violent temper – was knocking back drinks with the notoriously moody and eccentric Deep Purple guitarist Ritchie Blackmore. Bonham, Eddie later recalled, looked the Van Halen brothers up and down before dismissing them with a simple: 'Who *are* you? Fuck off?'[15] It was one more sign of a change in tone and atmosphere that had twisted the Strip into a kaleidoscopic, self-obsessed, sealed-off little world fuelled by jealousy and competition, much of it driven by the over-indulgence of rock stars. 'If peace and love were the buzz words for the sixties', Danny Sugerman observed in *Wonderland Avenue*, his memoir of life in the Los Angeles music industry, 'then decadence, at least in rock'n'roll Southern California, was the pronounced good of the new era dawning.'[16]

Van Halen's long spell at unfashionable Gazzarri's, although right next door to the bars and clubs where the hip and the famous would hang out, placed them distinctly off the 'happening' map. They were just another bar band. This would have much to do with the fact that the bands that Bill Gazzarri hired were less the stars of the show than they were the stand-in for a jukebox; which is to say, they provided entertainment to order. Phast Phreddie Patterson, a musician-turned-journalist from those days, recalled that the venue had, from the 1970s to the '90s, fallen into the security of hiring cover bands. 'Aside from Van Halen', he wrote,

> as a rule very few good bands played there . . . Gazzarri's was a very square club that featured bands playing mediocre metal, quasi funk, doodling disco or K-Mart styled New Wave.[17]

In fact, even in the 1960s it had been considered one of the more 'square' clubs on the Strip where, with few exceptions, unthreatening performers like Trini Lopez and Johnny Rivers had played to 'undemanding nightlifers'.[18] Only the fact that The Doors had been something of a house band there for a time in the mid-1960s could have lent the club – in the Dog Days of 1974 – the feel of a stepping stone to better things. But the truth remained that no band played at Gazzarri's if they could get into the better venues in Hollywood – The Whisky, The Roxy and The Troubadour.

Over hundreds of nights that unwound down to Van Halen's real zero hour in 1977 – more than three years into a future that might have seemed like it would never appear – they would occupy Gazzarri's small, elevated stage, which placed the performer *behind* the waist-high metal bars of a fence that, in many ways, kept them in their place. It was symbolic of imprisonment within the Hollywood Top 40 grind, and they would duly play several sets a night, every night. Flanked by mirror balls on either side of the stage, a large sign hovered above the heads of the band – but it didn't read 'Van Halen'; instead it proclaimed simply, 'Gazzarri's Hollywood'. Although Gazzarri – like a number of other figures – would later claim to have 'discovered' Van Halen he didn't seem to know much about exactly who these four young guys were. In those days Gazzarri left the running of the club to Greg Ladanyi (who later achieved prominence as a record producer in the 1980s for Warren Zevon, Jackson Browne and others), but still liked to add the occasional personal touch to the running of the club. After particularly successful nights – that is, when a lot of cash had passed over the bar – he approached Roth to give him a bonus to share with the band. 'Here, Van,' he would say (as if he was 'Van', like Van Morrison): 'here's an extra twenty bucks.'

Back in early 1974, however, as Van Halen began their first series of dates on the Strip on 4 April – spread over two weeks, initially – the sound of rock'n'roll was somewhat muted in Hollywood. While gigantic billboards advertised albums and forthcoming concerts by artists whose songs Van Halen would sometimes incorporate into their Gazzarri's set – Mott the Hoople, David Bowie and Elton John – what little action there was seemed to be elsewhere. At The Whisky A Go Go, for instance, the already well-known Captain Beefheart and the Magic Band were playing a series of dates, while next door at the Roxy Theatre, just a few metres along from Gazzarri's, was *The Rocky Horror Show* (featuring soon-to-be phenomenon Meat Loaf in a leading role). The latter show perhaps stood as evidence of rock'n'roll's declining presence in Hollywood and was, in fact, only one of a number of musical

'Put a little fun in your life – try dancing' were the by-words of Gazzarri's On the Strip, pictured here in 1973. Van Halen – following in the footsteps of The Doors in the mid-1960s – would become the house-band at Gazzarri's in early 1974, and played multiple sets per night for several nights a week until late 1976.

theatre productions during this period that found a home on the Strip. Elsewhere that weekend – at Ontario Speedway in San Bernardino County – was where most Los Angeles teenagers and most of Van Halen's hometown Pasadena crowd might have been found, at the California Jam festival. A crowd of over 200,000 watched the likes of the Eagles, Black Sabbath, Emerson, Lake and Palmer, and Deep Purple perform. There, Eddie's future adversary, Ritchie Blackmore – enraged that he had been forced out of his trailer and onstage before the sun had set – was jousting with something else that was in his way, an ABC TV camera. Luckily the camera got to record its own demise, as the guitarist methodically set about destroying it, by plunging the headstock of his Fender Stratocaster repeatedly into its intrusive eye.[19] But, since Jimi Hendrix and The Who had tried to out-smash each other at 1967's Monterey Pop festival, this all probably seemed just another part of the show – time for a hot dog.

In West Hollywood during the 1970s the real rock stars hung around at The Troubadour, or in the exclusive bar upstairs from The Roxy Theatre, which was aptly named On the Rox. Inside it wasn't unusual to find the likes of Keith Moon, Alice Cooper and John Lennon – then on his infamous eighteen-month-long 'lost weekend' – getting uproariously drunk together. In fact, in mid-April of 1974 *Rolling Stone* magazine had just run the story of the forcible ejection of Lennon from The Troubadour club on Santa Monica Boulevard for behaviour said to be more fitting to an Irish pub – insults were hurled, punches thrown and glasses smashed. In a sign of these times, perhaps, Lennon had, in Barney Hoskyns's words, 'rampaged through Hollywood like a one-man hurricane'.[20]

But in the midst of the less-than-vibrant music scene, the most distinctive eruption of teen culture since 1967 was catered to inside the four walls of Rodney Bingenheimer's English Disco, which was located on Sunset Boulevard, but just off the Strip far enough to signify its real distance from the social world of venues like The Troubadour.

Rodney Bingenheimer, who would come to play a significant part in Van Halen's emergence from the rut that was Gazzarri's, had been around on the 1960s Hollywood scene and in many ways represented the bridge between the two decades – if not the changes that had taken place at both ends. He had once served, in Danny Sugerman's words, as an 'aide-de-camp to Sonny and Cher and as Davy Jones's stand-in on *The Monkees*', but was also a plugger for a number of Hollywood record companies.[21] During a 1971 stay in London, when he was acting in a promotional capacity for the then little-known David Bowie, Bingenheimer had been inspired by the emerging UK Glam Rock scene and, with Bowie's encouragement, returned to Hollywood to open his now infamous club in 1972.

The English Disco was concealed during the daytime behind an inauspicious looking shop front that had a single wooden door for an entrance – it might have been a hardware shop. At night, though, flashing light bulbs illuminated the words 'Rodney Bingenheimer's' on the main sign. Inside the latest hits by the likes of T-Rex, David Bowie and The Sweet provided a soundtrack to which glammed-up, platform-shoed teenagers danced. They, in so many ways, were the stars of this place. A Warholian touch on Bingenheimer's part was to hang the walls on the dance floor with screens that played a slideshow of the teenage regulars, who appeared next to visiting stars from the UK or regulars like Iggy Pop.

One notable witness and insider was Hollywood pop music hustler, Kim Fowley – once described memorably as 'the *éminence grise* of rock'n'roll pimpdom' by Barney Hoskyns. Fowley had already been around and seen the ups and downs of the previous fifteen years in Hollywood. Many years later he recalled that Bingenheimer's place was distinguished most of all by a unique kind of culture; a new and more determined lunge towards teenage decadence. It was the routine sex, drugs and rock'n'roll, but with the addition of a setting in which teenage groupies became the bait for the many stars who visited the club, whether they were there to gawp in amazement or for more lurid reasons.[22] They, and the scene – 'the circus of the LA queens' – were captured by Led Zeppelin in 'Sick Again', a song that appeared on *Physical Graffiti* (1975). It told of the 'painted ladies' that were 'not yet sixteen' throwing themselves at the rock stars of the day.

Inside The English Disco events were often literally overseen from a raised seating area above the dance floor by none other than the stars who provided its soundtrack, including 'the visiting Led Zeppelins or Bowies or Bolans' who could be found sitting alongside ambitious young groupies.[23] Elvis Presley even visited Bingenheimer's club on one occasion to check the scene out for himself.[24] Danny Sugerman, a publicist for Elektra Records who was then acting chiefly as chaperone for one of Hollywood's more unpredictable characters of the time – the permanently zonked Iggy Pop – summed up the decadent atmosphere in an image of disengaged oblivion as he recalled 'sitting in a VIP booth getting wrecked on champagne, snorting cocaine out of a vial behind the menu', all the while casually catching glimpses of the action on the dance floor below.[25]

Given the rock star misbehaviour taking place elsewhere in Hollywood – what with John Lennon making headlines for his drunken revelry – it perhaps seemed that the night life of the Strip was descending into an extended bout of alcohol- and cocaine-fuelled self-destruction. If Iggy Pop, for instance, was not to be found inside The English Disco or The Whisky A Go Go, there was every chance that he'd be found outside some-where, lying in the street and perhaps clad in the dress he had taken to wearing around Hollywood at the time. Witnesses recall seeing him on the sidewalk, hitching up his skirt at passers-by to reveal the 'family jewels' (as he was apt to do onstage, too, as it happens), as he slugged from a bottle of cheap wine.[26] Ray Manzarek, The Doors' keyboard player who was then trying to put a band together with Iggy Pop – or Jim, as he usually called him (Iggy's real name was Jim Osterberg) – recalls appearing at the Hollywood police station to bail the singer out, after the police had picked him up for vagrancy, only to see a figure emerge clad in the infamous dress:

I looked at him and said, 'Jim, is that a woman's dress?'
And Iggy said, 'No, Ray, I beg to differ. This is a man's
dress.' Danny and I grabbed him and said, 'You asshole,
c'mon, let's get the hell out of here.' And you could hear
the cops kind of smirking and kind of guffawing and stifling
laughs and shaking their heads as out go Sugerman and
Manzarek, with Iggy Pop in the middle.[27]

With the Hollywood sign a near ruin, and rock'n'roll decadence
in the air, the downward spiral was summed up . . . Kim Fowley
later recounted, in the blasé attitude that seemed to prevail,

Joan Jett told me she was walking past The English Disco
one night when someone had just been murdered in front
of it and she could still hear 'Devil Gate Drive' playing
inside. She said to herself, 'This is Rock'n'Roll!'[28]

While Bingenheimer's club played the kind of music that
served as an antidote to the new rock aristocracy of the so-called
'cocaine cowboys' – many of whom lived behind Sunset Strip in
the hills of Laurel Canyon, and whose mellow offerings had come
to dominate music on the West Coast and the airwaves beyond
– it was a short-lived home for Glam, and closed in 1974, barely
two years after opening. The reality was that country rock and
the singer-songwriter scene ruled the day and dominated the
West Coast record industry. It meant, in Fowley's words, that the
likes of Linda Rondstadt and the Eagles appeared all of a sudden
to be the 'Vanderbilts and Rockefellas of rock and roll'.[29] For
many, Fowley included, it seemed that rock'n'roll on the Strip
had passed a point of no return.

Such was the Hollywood that formed the cultural backdrop to
Van Halen's arrival in the spring of 1974. With live bands appearing

extremely infrequently, if at all, at Bingenheimer's English Disco, and more established clubs like The Whisky A Go Go and the Roxy usually featuring more or less established bands, there were few outlets for any unsigned band playing their own material. Even The Whisky, the heart of the Sunset Strip scene since the early 1960s, eventually turned its back on live rock'n'roll, first in favour of soul and R'n'B acts (because they were deemed less likely to attract troublesome crowds) and later, like the Roxy, to host musical theatre productions with titles like *El Grande de Coca Cola*, which tended to run for extended periods of time.

For a band like Van Halen – yet to record and unable to trade on their own songs – it was necessary to earn their living and pay their dues by performing entire sets of cover songs. The situation was not so unusual – playing other artists' songs had always been a feature of gaining a foothold in popular music since the earliest days of rock'n'roll and only changed significantly in the wake of Bob Dylan and The Beatles and the elevation of the idea of the singer and performer as a writer of songs. But in the 1970s, in the age of a certain kind of singer-songwriter authenticity – mellow, acoustic guitar-based songs, confessional lyrics – things had changed. Now, it was easy to be seen as lacking in cool to be playing Top 40 hits, especially if you didn't actually write them. In that era, in fact, very few established bands or performers continued to play songs other than those they wrote themselves, as the money and kudos to be earned from being a songwriter became clear – Bruce Springsteen was one notable exception to the rule, and in his case the dozens of cover tunes he performed were left off his records and reserved for his marathon live shows.

In Van Halen, the creative wellspring was always Eddie Van Halen. While David Lee Roth had reputedly been for a time an acoustic guitar troubadour, playing at Pasadena's Ice House club as a solo performer before joining up with the Van Halen brothers, he was no singer-songwriter in the 1970s mould. In fact, the acoustic guitar might have seemed to be incongruous alongside the Bowie-style brush-cut he sported, and he played blues songs. Roth also possessed ears that were too easily seduced by pop radio, and by soul and disco, to be drawn to the rhinestone cowboys – all of which, in some way, helped the band to source enough suitable material to keep eking out a living at clubs like Gazzarri's at a time when new bands were being starved out of existence by the lack of outlets for live music in Hollywood.

What club owners really wanted – as Eddie told the *Los Angeles Times* in 1977 – was thirsty customers. They wanted their patrons to keep drinking, which meant a constant supply of danceable tunes that somewhat reflected the action on the charts – that's what made people move and got them into working up a sweat and a thirst. 'We were supposed to make sure the people got into the bar,' Eddie said, 'not into the band.'[30] And so it remained. But as it remained so, it seems clear that Roth's influence within the band increased as he cajoled the others into moulding a dance-friendly set list that would keep the bookings steady until they had more of an opportunity to drop their own material into the act.

While Van Halen may, at the time, have felt that this was merely a necessary dues-paying period that would lead on to the chance of making their own records, it nonetheless saw them develop in ways that a band not forced into such an existence would not have done: which is to say, the musical entity they became as they embarked upon their recording career a few years later was stamped with this pop influence due to the historical accident of having to exist in the denuded rock'n'roll environment of the mid-1970s Sunset Strip. On the other hand, it meant that they were able to become – if and when a song demanded it – a three- or four-part vocal group simply because it was the only way they could adapt certain songs. Horn-driven R'n'B numbers like James Brown's 'Cold Sweat', or tunes like The Isley Brothers' 'It's Your Thing' or 'Fopp' by the Ohio Players, required a bit more than guitar, bass and drums. The lack of horns and keyboards were covered with background vocals or by Eddie's ability to use the guitar to fill out space.[31] This is not to say that they managed to pull it off very convincingly. The evidence of bootleg recordings tends to reveal that while the Van Halen of the mid-1970s were a tight and well-rehearsed outfit, they were better at covering songs like 'Twist and Shout' (Beatles style), or doing a convincing impression of the then popular James Gang, than they were at doing dance-funk tunes. But in those years Van Halen – like Top 40 club predecessors such as Trini Lopez or Johnny Rivers – morphed into a kind of human jukebox, with a repertoire of some 200 songs at their disposal.

'We'd turn on the radio to hear what the music fashion was that week and take it from there', Mike Anthony said. 'Horn bands like KC and the Sunshine Band were big then, so we learned all their stuff.'[32] Later the band would record a succession of cover tunes, including two songs by The Kinks ('You Really Got Me' and 'Where Have All the Good Times Gone'), which came directly from the experience of these early years. As Roth recalled, such was their repertoire that they might have recorded any of six Kinks tunes that figured in their live shows:

> Back in our bar days, I bought a double album from K-Tel or something that had 30 Kinks tunes on it. We learned all of one side and played them into the dirt during the club gigs, twice a night each one, because they sounded good and they were great to dance to.[33]

Van Halen's Hollywood was, as a result of the years stuck in this club scene, far removed not only from the 1960s, but also from later developments in the early 1980s, when a rash of new bands appeared on the Sunset Strip, following in the wake of the new glam metal bands, led by Mötley Crüe. The difference between the 1970s and the '80s is marked by the fact that, in the 1970s, there was no 'demographic' for an aspiring band playing the Sunset Strip clubs to chase and no real record company interest in what was going on. By 1987, when Guns N' Roses released *Appetite for Destruction*, they were, Barney Hoskyns suggests, 'just one of a hundred identikit LA bands with lion manes, loud guitars and bicep artwork courtesy of Sunset Strip Tattoo'.[34] Van Halen were no less isolated from the predominant country rock and singer-songwriters of the early 1970s. That was a scene supported by significant changes in the record industry, particularly in the nurturing relationship that some labels and their owners now professed, with the likes of David Geffen's Asylum Records, Elektra and Warner Brothers signing up 'artists' and not mere fodder for the pop charts.

For Van Halen, the only goal was to keep playing – but it meant creating an audience. A crucial characteristic of the musical culture of those times is that popular music was far from the many-headed monster it is today. 'Rock'n'roll', as a descriptive term, applied to almost every kind of music that was presumed to appeal to young people during a period that went roughly from the mid-1950s to the mid-1970s. In retrospect, the fate of that term is rather akin to disappearing political allegiances to nations or ideologies, which began to be eroded by a tide of identity politics and subcultural particularity in recent decades. Following such wider social and cultural changes, popular music today is about identity in a much more particular sense, and now characterized by a proliferation of sub-genres that seem to exist, as such, not only to cater to par-ticular tastes ('indie', 'grunge', 'post-rock', 'death metal' and so on), but to service more effectively the niche markets that have, as a consequence, been well identified by those who are in the business of selling music.

That is not to say that rock'n'roll, in the 1970s, was about anything essentially different – it was, for instance, no less of a commodity than it had always been at the level of the Top 40. Yet to contrast these eras is to reveal that there is a deal more cynicism in the targeting of popular music today; that it is more about giving the people what they already know that they want. In some regards, therefore, music and musicians, even when they were compelled to spend years playing the songs of others, existed in a freer environment. It is for those kinds of reasons that 'rock'n'roll' came to be associated more with a kind of attitude to life than simply a musical genre.

It was thus that Van Halen could decide, one night in 1975, to target Bob Marley's audience at The Roxy as their own future fans, handing out flyers and stuffing them under car windscreen wipers.[35] After all, didn't the cover of Marley's *Catch a Fire* album show him smoking a huge spliff? Wasn't Bob Marley as rock'n'roll as anybody else? On that night Roth watched Keith Richards and Ringo Starr enter The Roxy as he waited outside with his glue and posters stuffed under his jacket, ready to plaster the walls when the coast was clear.[36]

Van Halen continued to exist on their own little Hollywood island until 1976, when the sudden emergence of a host of new bands, inspired by the DIY attitude of the New York and London punk scenes, appeared in Los Angeles in need of places to play. They were united by a determination to avoid the Top 40 grind and a desire to perform their own material. As it happened, almost everything that appeared in that time seemed to at some point be tagged with the 'punk' label; it was the biggest – the only – wave heading for shore, and it was carrying everything that was apparently not fixed to the Los Angeles music industry along with it.

As Barney Hoskyns suggests in *Waiting for the Sun*, his history of the Los Angeles music scene, while Van Halen could be separated from these new bands because they had been around longer, they had – in attitude, if not much more – 'one foot in the Sunset glam-punk scene of 1974'.[37] Although, as a glance at the sleeve of Van Halen's debut album – which was photographed in late 1977 or early 1978 – reveals, this was a foot that still wore its platforms proudly. But the 'Sunset glam-punk' connection also explains a lot, since Van Halen ended up benefiting from the support of two of the principal instigators of the new Sunset Strip scene – Kim Fowley and Rodney Bingenheimer – the lynchpins of the earlier glam scene.

By mid-1976 they both thought that the sudden emergence of new bands inspired by the punk ethos created an opportunity to remake the spirit of the mid-1960s Sunset Strip – that is, to foster a culture that was driven not by the old ways of the record industry but by the music of the young.[38]

For Fowley, the enemies of rock'n'roll lived up in the canyons. They had, in league with the record labels, re-positioned the music business in favour of introspective singer-songwriters and, in personal terms, it posed a threat to his existence as a publisher and song hustler. The plain fact was that any bands that might record Fowley songs – or employ him as a producer – helped pay his rent. His need to hustle gave him a certain motivation to seek out new talent, which, he believed, was the only thing that kept the music scene from stagnating. In his estimation, Laurel Canyon and the Hollywood hills – the retreat of those who had 'made it' – represented the antithesis of the values of the Strip. Life in the rural surroundings of the hills, like the music made by the new kings and queens of country rock, was a dead bore that could only be sustained by what Fowley saw as the coke-fuelled insularity of rock music as big business.

In 1974 Fowley released *Animal God of the Streets,* an album whose title alone seemed to pitch him at the opposite pole to the musicians who lived in the canyons. Always aggressive in his estimation of his contemporaries, Fowley considered their retreat to the hills evidence enough that they were 'incapable of eyeball-to-eyeball hustling on Sunset Boulevard'.[39] But, of course, the truth now was that they didn't need to be. They had the likes of David Geffen to do it on their behalf.

Fowley, though, had been around on the Hollywood music scene long enough to think that a change in fortunes could be engineered. He had already acted widely as a manager and publisher, as well as writing and producing songs for artists too numerous to detail, and cut some great pop records himself. One of these songs was the great, but resoundingly obscure 45 B-side, 'Twenty-Five Hours a Day' by the pseudonymous 'Jimmy Juke-box' (1973), which itself captures the spirit of the kind of songs one might have found echoing through the door of Bingenheimer's English Disco between 1972 and 1974. It recites the virtues of a litany of rock'n'roll greats, before landing in the repetitive chant of a chorus that celebrates the sum of all values to be in the near narcotic 'hit' of an eternal moment that might extend the day itself in some kind of homage to being young.

If to be young was to crave 25 hours in a day, as Fowley would have it, then it also meant wanting more; more than what was on offer, more of life. 'Most of today's rock is controlled, manufactured and performed by people over 30 who are not rebelling against anything', Fowley said in 1976. The way forward was to seize on the 'swaggering, obnoxious, fighting-back spirit' of young bands who were starting to crop up across the city. The one song Fowley co-wrote with Van Halen – recorded by the band in 1977, but never officially released – was titled, in typically Fowley-esque fashion, 'Young and Wild'. It was around this time that his involvement with new Los Angeles bands was being noted in the press. In an interview with the *Los Angeles Times* he explained that his position as a hustler on the music scene was almost the only way to avoid the fact of not fitting in – socially and culturally – anywhere else:

I had polio [as a child] and I was paralyzed and I was ugly, so I had to overcompensate. I was too young for politics. I

opposite: David Lee Roth backstage at The Whisky A Go Go, May 1977.

wasn't strong enough for athletics. I wasn't pure enough
to be religious. I wasn't inferior enough to be a criminal,
so what else was there?[40]

This sometime 'Jimmy Jukebox' was, as Harvey Kubernik noted,
something of a 'human jukebox' himself, but one whose interests
extended into all corners of the industry and its often murky
shenanigans. These ranged from 'social politics, room-working,
creativity [and] talent-discovery', to the 'country club rules, religion
(not as faith, but as entry and business opportunity), competition,
betrayal, and scamming'. And on and on the list could go.[41] Although
he never attained the position of a Phil Spector, Fowley had amassed,
even by the mid-1970s, songwriting, publishing and production
credits on possibly tens of dozens of hit records (some big hits,
others not), including the Hollywood Argyles' 'Alley Oop', a US
number one hit single in 1961. When Led Zeppelin took up resi-
dence in Hollywood during their American tours in the early 1970s,
the one Los Angeles music figure that singer Robert Plant wanted
to meet was not Neil Young, not Joni Mitchell, but Fowley – the
man behind the Hollywood Argyles.

While Bingenheimer, Fowley's erstwhile partner in all this,
had to watch his English Disco go under as a consequence of the
gradual waning of the English Glam Rock that was its main
reason for existing, he was, by mid-1976, hosting a radio show on
the local station KROQ. He also fired off monthly gossip columns
for the long-defunct music magazine *Phonograph Record Magazine*
(among other publications). Under a by-line that read, 'Vicious
Dirt, Rumors and Scandals from Hollywood', the reader would
find vignettes from his Warhol-esque diary of happenings and
parties, which usually revolved around the activities of visiting
pop luminaries.

opposite: The Mumps, May 1977, one of the many punk/new wave bands that shared the
bill with Van Halen during 1976–7.

In the aftermath of a Van Halen show in Pasadena, Bingenheimer ensured that they were booked into The Starwood night
club, where they would be given a chance to air their own
material to an audience not there for a dance contest. In the
December issue of *Phonograph Record Magazine* in 1976, Bingenheimer – an unapologetic groupie – regaled readers with tales of
the Hollywood scene, including a party with a visiting Patti Smith,
from which – he reported – 'your handsome, but by no means
hand-me-down Prince is still trying to recuperate'. Commenting
on Smith's role in the punk revolution, he suggested that Los
Angeles was birthing a scene of its own to match New York or
London. Among the bands on the 'punk scene', he noted, was
Van Halen.[42] Fowley also talked them up as part of a new wave of
'punk rock, street-rock, heavy metal' bands in a *Los Angeles Times*
feature in 1976.[43]

It was at The Starwood that Bingenheimer's guests Gene
Simmons and Paul Stanley, of the band KISS, first saw Van Halen.
Soon after this encounter Simmons, now well known as a
determined businessman, took the band into the Village Recorders
in Los Angeles to cut, Eddie later said, 'the world's most expensive
demo tape' – paid for by Simmons. They later flew to New York
to do overdubs at Electric Ladyland studios, and audition for
Simmons's manager, Bill Aucoin. In the end, it all came to nothing – Aucoin wasn't interested, so Simmons reluctantly waved
Van Halen goodbye. While that tape has surfaced and been in
circulation for decades now, at the time the band seemed to have
been left only with a cheap cassette dub of the master: 'on top
of not having the [original] tape', Eddie said in 1979, 'we didn't
know where it was. We didn't know anyone. We just kept playing
the LA area – everywhere.'[44]

By early 1977, some of the new Hollywood bands that belonged
to the blossoming scene that Fowley and Bingenheimer had been
talking up had organized themselves under the name 'Radio Free

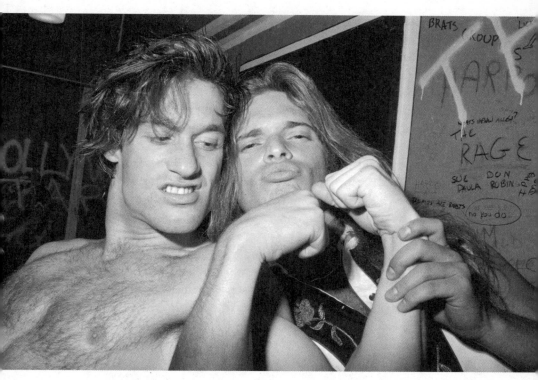

Lance Loud (left), lead singer with The Mumps, pictured backstage at The Whisky A Go Go with David Lee Roth, May 1977.

Hollywood' to try to break into the Strip's more established venues. These bands – whose names included The Pop!, The Motels and The Dogs – were crucial in creating an environment that also, as Barney Hoskyns says, 'opened doors for bands as seemingly incompatible' as Van Halen and Tom Petty and the Heartbreakers, who had recently moved to Hollywood from Florida.[45] Fowley also put together bands for The Whisky A Go Go and alerted the club's booker Marshall Berle (who would become Van Halen's first manager) to the band's existence.

Van Halen first appeared at The Whisky in early December 1976 under a 'Kim Fowley Presents' banner, sharing the bill with Venus and The Razorblades (a Fowley-managed band). In that month alone Van Halen played six shows at The Whisky A Go Go, and later throughout 1977 they would return to the venue several times a month, performing around 30 times in total during the year. In early 1977 the *Los Angeles Times* had them tagged as 'the slickest and most commercially promising' band on the Hollywood scene.[46] But just as they had sailed between earlier fads and fashions on the Strip, they quickly outpaced the punk scene of 1976–7 they had accidentally found themselves in the midst of. As Eddie said, they were never really a Hollywood band anyway – they were from Pasadena.

Back home in Pasadena, however, as Chris Holmes – boyhood friend of Eddie, follower of early 1970s Van Halen and later guitar player for the notorious WASP – said, as soon as the band signed with Warner Bros Records in 1977 an outbreak of jealousy ensured that 'everybody in Pasadena hated 'em'.[47]

3 THE GOLDEN DREAM, CALIFORNIA

There is a golden haze over the land – the dust of gold is in the air – and the atmosphere is magical and mirrors many tricks, deceptions, and wondrous visions.

– Carey McWilliams, *California, The Great Exception*

Since the mid-nineteenth century 'California' had been an idea as much as it was the name for a distinctive part of the USA. It has, for more than a century now, been bound up with a history of exaggeration and boosterism, and particularly with the representations of its own myth-making industry – Hollywood. As a land of dreams, the wondrous visions that came to be associated with it would reach far beyond the United States, impressing – in particular – young would-be consumers of the Californian ideal. The writer Dana Polan recalls, as a child, watching a cartoon in which a gang of comic characters are seen to trudge through torrential rain en route to California, then (as now) cast as the Promised Land. During their journey they were seen to endure a 'downpour complemented by intensely dark skies and ear-shattering thunder', but 'when they reached the border (literally a line in the terrain) the Californian side was instantly revealed as pure sunshine, a land of beautiful and resplendent weather'.[1]

Like stepping from a black-and-white world into Technicolor, it was the most rudimentary example of California's mixing of the real and the idealized. In such apparently unremarkable visions the aptly named 'Golden State' is presented as the antidote to the nagging disappointments of reality. In fact, the power of its myths offer a testament to how familiar the mere *idea* of California has become, and to how it was so easily absorbed into the cultural consciousness of generations of hopeful migrants who set out to discover it for themselves.

In numerous ways that remain in accord with Dana Polan's cartoon experience, a California that was as often imaginary as it was real came to be equated with ideas of perfection; it was 'an Edenic utopia . . . an exotic tropical paradise, as [well as] the ultimate cash prize and end point of Manifest Destiny'.[2] In practical terms, the status of this garden of Eden as variously a myth, dream or reality ultimately did not matter because – as we know from the tricks used in product advertising – the promise of future perfection can become a self-fulfilling prophecy. Buying into California at the level of the myth already meant that old ways would be discarded and inherited traditions likely be refused. California represented pure future – a history unwritten, a paradise yet to be exploited. It was a new and younger future as against a history that already claimed the future as its own. All of which is to say, the combination of the idea of California with a *desire* to be Californian, fostered – historically speaking – a newer kind of mindset; a determination to live in the present that was more marked than in any other part of the USA.[3]

Southern California, in particular, embodied the 'sunshine state' of the early boosters of the nineteenth century – the likes of Charles Lummis, founder of a periodical devoted to promoting the region that went by the unequivocal title *Land of Sunshine*.

In Pasadena, birthplace of Van Halen (although not the birthplace of any of its members), the myth of California was, for many, perpetuated in what actually looked every inch 'the garden spot of the earth'.[4] There its fortunate dwellers might wander casually from the leisured domesticity of sun-kissed afternoons in lush gardens of exotic plants and citrus trees to a more untamed, yet benign, wilderness to the west of the city, known as the Arroyo Seco. In the words of the Californian historian Kevin Starr, it was 'thick with sycamores, oak, willows, alder, tangled thickets of wild

P-4   ARROYO SECO, COLORADO STREET BRIDGE, PASADENA, CALIFORNIA

Pasadena, 1920s.

grapes, clematis, and other flowering plants'.[5] This abundant 'garden California' became associated soon enough in the nineteenth century with a particular climate that, in the view of one visitor from the Old South, had an almost palpable force. 'Exaltation', he wrote to his family back home, 'is in the atmosphere.'[6]

Early settlers in the Pasadena area felt that the Mediterranean climate of what would come to be known as the Southland (marking it as distinct from the culture of cities in Northern California) ought to give birth to new ways of living – it wasn't merely to be the latest alluring destination one might aspire to forge a life in. The new Californians manifested their separation from the old and the unwanted in a proliferation of unconventional systems of belief – variously spiritual and lifestyle-related – which have continued to flourish in California.[7] 'I am told that the millennium has already begun in Pasadena', one resident, having grown weary of the city's burgeoning Bohemian influx, wrote to a friend in 1895, 'and that even now there are more sanctified cranks to the

acre than in any other town in America'.[8] The Theosophist Annie
Besant thought that the future of humanity rested in California's
example and that Pasadena was the 'source of the finest vibrations
in the world'.[9]

For Carey McWilliams, the author of numerous texts that
detail the scope and dimensions of the Californian landscape
and imagination, 'self-invention' was indeed the 'region's most
distinctive characteristic'.[10] David Lee Roth – a second-generation
Jewish Russian-American who would become some kind of
exemplar of the Californian way of life – was well aware that
the people who made up California had, in one way or another,
all arrived in this place to get away from the Old World; from
people telling them how to act and live, and what they could and
could not believe. This was one reason it became such a magnet
for so-called 'cranks', but also for freethinkers and bohemian
types. The importance of the belief in the possibilities of self-
invention helps us to understand, as McWilliams wrote, the State's
'fabled addiction to cults and cultists' whose visions of the new
world ranged from the transcendental and dangerously decadent
(Aleister Crowley was a resident of Pasadena for a while) to the
strange and sci-fi (L. Ron Hubbard's Scientology and the astral
loopiness of the Heaven's Gate cult of the 1990s both seem characteristically Californian). The more banal aspects of everyday
life and culture that spoke of this kind of self-invention were
manifested in what, to many outsiders, seemed to be rather
odd attitudes to diet, dress and even time; to how the days might
be divided up to best take advantage of Southern California's
unique climate.[11]

Grace Ellery Channing, an editor of Lummis's booster
periodical, *Land of Sunshine*, thought that Southern California
might, like Spain and Italy, those countries it was said most
to resemble in the faraway Mediterranean, even introduce the
midday siesta. This was the kind of idea, of course, that in itself

marked the state's uniqueness within the USA, representing an attitude to life that would seem to have been unthinkable in other parts of the country. One might point to the Northeast and Midwest, where life could be harsh due to their own climactic peculiarities, and where people had to adapt their life and culture to ends that suited local conditions – that is to say, place is arguably always important in the formation of beliefs and values. Within the vastness of the USA, California therefore came to be a kind of world in and of itself and, indeed, would give rise to an expression – 'Californian exceptionalism' – that marked its distinctive political and cultural tendencies.[12]

Between the era of Lummis, Channing – and the numerous other early champions of the California way of life – and the era that is the main concern of these ruminations, much had changed in the region, in Los Angeles and nearby Pasadena. A huge migration westwards had swollen the population of the state and saw Los Angeles emerge, after some false starts at the turn of the twentieth century, as a city-region whose sprawl by mid-century was so marked that it could be known as the home of sun, sea and surf, the capital of a global film industry, yet also be the largest industrial 'city' in the USA.[13] What arguably remained unchanged amid such large-scale social and demographic transformations was the *idea* of California. It was, as Mike Davis has said, 'a unique *state-nation* on the Pacific' – but also a state of mind.[14]

The 'many Californias', whatever form they took, unavoidably derived from the State's invented past; from ways of living that may have seemed to have sprung from nowhere, but which, in actuality, were formed from the co-mingling of many seemingly incompatible beliefs and practices that had found a place to flourish there as nowhere else. Thus, while new generations of Pasadenans might not have lived any longer in a city whose air was filled with the 'languorous perfume' of blossoming orange trees and 'peach, almond, apricot [and] poppy trees running right into the city' –

because they lived in a reality that was often more characterized by car fumes and the bustle of modernity – there was nonetheless born an attitude to life affected by the region's myths, which in turn conditioned the course of life, much like a secondary weather system setting the psychological, temperamental, climate.[15]

For many who arrived in Southern California during the twentieth century, of course, the reality often did not quite match up to the myth, which was long held to have been constructed on the back of exaggerated reports of Elysian virtues, as Carey McWilliams noted:

> In the eighties it began to be said that Southern Californians 'irrigate, cultivate and exaggerate'. Nor was it only the climate that was reported with some slight exaggeration. In particular the products of its soil, its Brobdingnagian vegetables loomed larger than life in the tourist reports. One reads of tomato vines nineteen feet high; of cabbage plants that grew twenty feet in the air; of strawberries so big they could only be consumed by three large bites, of cucumbers seven feet long.[16]

That was the 1880s. In the 1960s was it really any different when Jan and Dean sang to the world of 'Surf City', a place where there could be found *two girls for every boy*? They weren't taking a headcount, but reflecting that same tendency to exaggeration. It is perhaps no surprise, then, that Roth, transplanted into the Californian garden around the age of eight, would tell bemused journalists, 'everything you read is true – I live and breathe and do four times as much, four times as fast as anyone else'.[17] That Californian atmosphere, conjured up – in McWilliams's words – by 'many tricks, deceptions and wondrous visions', was what Roth had inhaled. Thus when he sang, as someone once observed, it wasn't so much singing as 'exuberating'.

Yet the real experience of waves of immigrants had shown that 'the Californian dream often mocks the reality'.[18] With slight exaggerations aside, gardens, sunshine and those boulevards lined with eucalyptus trees were perhaps a given in this place. But the promise of free fruit from ready-to-hand orange trees in one's backyard seemed to be, in the words of Eddie Van Halen – who arrived as a seven-year-old child from the Netherlands in 1962 – 'a crock of shit'. Eddie more than once said his family was *lured* to the 'land of opportunity', a phrase he seemed to almost spit out.[19] Thus it was not just to the place, but the myth that drew the Van Halen family far from their Netherlands home.

But whatever the disappointments may have been, Southern California's air of permissiveness, and the can-do attitude of those who had already prospered there, could still draw newcomers into the sunshine, and into its peculiar climate of mind.

A fundamental fact in this particular tale is that the future members of Van Halen, like millions of others before, were brought to Southern California (to the Pasadena-Altadena-Arcadia area) to find a new beginning – the Van Halens from Holland, Michael Anthony from the Midwest and Roth from Indiana (by way of New England and New York). What their families chose was the here and now – California as future – over the past.

All of that might help us to understand the fate of two young men who, if nothing else, were brought within proximity of each other entirely as the result of a series of coincidences. The dynamics of Van Halen's brand of rock'n'roll emerges from both a time and place, and as the result of the admixture of barely compatible elements.

For all the seeming inevitability of history, of what has been and passed, there was nothing certain about Roth and Eddie coming together; instead it was merely an accident that was the result, as Roth said, of the field clearing, leaving them facing one other. The Van Halens needed a new singer and Roth was the one credible guy in Pasadena who had the same desire to play music rather than working a normal job.[20]

Roth joined up with the Van Halen brothers in 1973, but that was really his second shot at it. Before that, sometime in 1972 or thereabouts, he had turned up on the doorstep of the Van Halen family home, located a few streets away from the fabled Route 66 that ran right through Pasadena, to say that he should be their new singer. He was sent away to learn some songs that the brothers played, songs he had no real passion for – by Cream or Black Sabbath – and returned a week later only to fail the audition. Years later – decades – Eddie was convinced that the singer still harboured a grudge about this verdict. After this first failed audition, Roth formed his own band, named Red Ball Jets. They and Eddie and Alex Van Halen's band (then going by the name of Mammoth) became local competitors. 'We were doing live Cream jams', Eddie said in 1995, implying that there was a gulf in technical ability between the two bands:

> they were up to 'Johnny B. Goode.' It was never about the music for him. It was about the show. We kinda became rival bands. People who liked us at one party would go to the next party, and I guess they'd throw stuff at him.[21]

If Eddie wasn't impressed by Roth's band, the animosity didn't get in the way of the fact that they would eventually need each other to realize the dream of self-invention that Southern California had encouraged in them. For all their differences, the passage of time since those early days seemed to show one thing: these were two individuals who seemed to be often alienated from their peers – Roth, in fact, was sent to therapy as a child because he refused to associate with his peers. Oddly the fact that both seemed almost out of time and out of joint, and ill at ease with the world they had created for themselves –

if not the world at large – may have been enough to keep them together.

The Van Halens had moved to California from Nijmegen, near the Dutch border with Germany, in 1962. It was perhaps not just for the positive (and, perhaps, mythical) benefits of the Southern Californian life, but maybe also because Eddie's and Alex's parents believed that a new start in the more culturally diverse setting of California might help avoid the likely difficulties of growing up as so-called 'Indos', the name given to those of mixed Dutch, Indonesian and Eurasian heritage (the Van Halens' father was Dutch and their mother Indonesian). The late 1950s and early '60s was a period in time when those seen as having such a mixed racial background were, according to many accounts, regarded as second-class Dutch citizens, both in the Netherlands and its colonial territories.[22]

While the accuracy of this perspective has been contested by some Dutch-Indonesians who remained in the Netherlands at the same time as large numbers migrated to California and other destinations, it is more widely held that Dutch society in the post-Second World War era engendered a sense of social cautiousness in those from an Indo background that, in itself, may have led to subconsciously self-imposed restrictions, curtailed ambitions and thus reduced life chances. Such attitudes may also be related to the historical status of those of mixed Dutch and Indonesian background within Indonesian society itself – there, they rarely rose, in occupational terms, to the highest level, or into roles or careers that would challenge a tendency to play safe. All of which was arguably a consequence of being caught, and visibly so, between the Dutch and the native Indonesian population.[23]

As it was, the first generation of Dutch-Indonesian immigrants to the Netherlands in the post-Second World War years numbered an estimated 180,000 people.[24] Among them would have been Eugenia van Beers, Eddie and Alex Van Halen's mother. Those

immigrants, in common with colonial migrants to a number of
other European countries, often faced a hostile social and cultural
climate that, as Mark Taylor Brinsfield has noted, took a generation
to mellow:

> Rather than warmly welcoming them as fellow Netherlanders,
> many Dutch people harboured against them an array of
> negative stereotypes which had been developed in the three
> and a half centuries of Dutch control over Indonesia. Indeed,
> the Dutch government had done everything possible to pre-
> vent most of the Eurasians from coming to the Netherlands
> in the first place.[25]

As Marlene De Vries puts it, for those Dutch Eurasians – regarded
as 'European' by native Indonesians – the 'mixture with Indonesian
blood' symbolized to their new Dutch hosts in the Netherlands,
'kinship to a race that was, consciously or unconsciously, considered inferior'.[26]

It was for such reasons that California – as the ideal of
a future life free from the past – was seen, by people from all
over the world, as the land of opportunity. By the early 1960s
Southern California would become home to the second largest
Dutch-Eurasian population in the world.[27] Before arriving in
the USA in 1962, the Van Halens already had relatives settled in
California – members of the van Beers family. They, along with
the Catholic Church, would have been the likely sponsors of the
family's emigration. Although California was a more ethnically
diverse culture than the Netherlands of the late 1950s and early
'60s, the Van Halens still stood out as ethnic misfits – initially
they spoke no English, which made life at school difficult, and
at home they spoke Dutch because their parents continued to
do so.

Eddie's and Alex's father, Jan, had been a professional musician, playing clarinet and saxophone in a number of orchestras and jazz bands in the Netherlands. In Pasadena, however, he had to hold down a handful of menial jobs to keep the family afloat. He walked six miles a day, Eddie recalled,

> from Pasadena, where we lived, to the Arcadia Methodist Hospital to wash dishes because he couldn't make it playing music . . . [but] he would gig on weekends playing proms and bar mitzvahs, anything he could get.[28]

One can only assume that he was reminded daily of what he had left behind as he approached an incongruous windmill atop the roof of the Van De Kamp coffee house that sat right next to Arcadia Methodist Hospital. Their menus were even adorned with Dutch maidens represented in national costume.

In the evening or on weekends he would dress up, in the lederhosen of Germany and the Alpines, to play with a polka band around the San Bernardino area. By the mid- to late 1960s, Alex Van Halen – almost two years older than Eddie – was there behind him on drums.

Eddie's route to the guitar began, as was the case with so many others of his generation, with the so-called 'British Invasion' bands of the early to mid-1960s: The Dave Clark Five, The Beatles and The Kinks. But later he became a fan of Southern California surf rock, particularly guitar instrumentals like 'Pipeline' by The Chantays, and 'Wipeout' by The Surfaris. 'Walk Don't Run', The Ventures' surf instrumental of 1963, was the first song he learned on guitar. The percussive opening chords of the guitar got under his skin so much that he would spend days on end – before he knew how to do anything else – playing the descending chord run. The influence of surf guitar and its continuous, often dramatic-sounding lead lines on Eddie's playing is not usually remarked upon, but is evident in a number of Van Halen songs that don't conform to the blues-derived structures of much rock guitar playing. The clearest example of this is perhaps 'Loss of Control' (1980), which – instrumentally, at least – might be the soundtrack to surfers breaking on the waves and crashing amid the spindrift. Other songs that, instrumentally, would fit within the surf rock genre include 'Romeo Delight' (1980) 'Sinners Swing!' (1981) and 'Top Jimmy' (1983).

While Eddie's much-noted obsession with Eric Clapton never resulted in imitation, it was such that, in late 1970, just short of his sixteenth birthday, he spent most of a concert by Clapton's new band, Derek and the Dominos, spying on the guitarist's technique from the audience with the aid of a small pair of binoculars he brought along especially for the occasion. With this enhanced gaze, he would see and hear a Clapton apparently possessed of some demon as he pushed his wah-wah-driven Fender Stratocaster to a screaming pitch of intensity that was entirely out of keeping with the more sedate playing on his recently released *Layla and Other Assorted Love Songs* album.[29] Eddie, already convinced that he would spend his life playing music, nonetheless had no idea that evening, as he spied Clapton's fingers from row six of the theatre through his little binoculars, that just five years later, he would be occupying this same stage – Pasadena's Civic Auditorium – with his own band.

At home Eddie would develop forensic methods appropriate to the task of getting to the root of Clapton's famed tone and feel; by easing the turntable of his record player down to 16 rpm, slowing down time, he could figure out what notes were being played – allowing him to disappear deep into the grooves of tunes like 'Strange Brew' and 'I'm So Glad'. Years later, in a tape-recorded interview with the journalist Lisa Robinson, he launched into an impromptu version of Cream's 'Crossroads' that matched Clapton's

opposite: Eddie Van Halen, May 1977.

playing in almost every little detail – proof, if nothing else, that years of intensive scrutiny and practice had left an indelible mark on him.

By 1973, Eddie and Alex Van Halen were renting space at a communal house in North Pasadena known as the Hanky Hacienda – which was described later by the *Los Angeles Times* as a 'rock'n'roll den of iniquity'.[30] It served as the home and HQ of local Pasadena legends Snotty Scotty and the Hankies. Soon the Van Halens and Roth were rehearsing there with a bass player named Mark Stone, whose fondness for building LSD molecules was such that he would eventually quit the band to study chemistry.

Going under the name Mammoth, at that time they were playing anywhere that would have them, from bowling alleys and high school gyms to Magic Mountain, an amusement park in Valencia to the north of Los Angeles. Ultimately, though, they would become more associated with a phenomenon that was arguably peculiar to the social climate and environment of 1970s Southern California.

In 1974 the US government had lowered the legal age for alcohol consumption to eighteen. Perhaps as a result of such liberalization, San Bernardino County saw the growth of large outdoor parties, with alcohol and drugs circulating freely among (often large) crowds of teenagers. Growing from modest origins in gatherings centred around the pool houses of large family homes – where a record player probably provided the only musical entertainment – into events that featured local bands putting on full-blown concerts, these occasions would provide Roth and the Van Halen brothers their earliest opportunities to develop as a stage band.

Before joining Mammoth, Roth had been observing the brothers and noting that they perhaps lacked something in the way of stagecraft; he later recalled them standing around between songs smoking and chatting with their girlfriends at the side of the stage, ignoring the audience. 'They wore Levi cords with the boxer shorts stickin' out and a T-shirt, and just sort of stood there', he later recalled – 'like Nirvana', some twenty-odd years later.[31] Eddie, according to Roth, would do Alvin Lee's turn from the *Woodstock* movie, playing 'Goin' Home' at high speed.[32] The repertoire was otherwise made up of the popular hard rock of the day – The Who's *Live At Leeds* (apparently they had been known to play it from beginning to end), Deep Purple or more obscure bands like Budgie and Captain Beyond.

In late 1973 one of the early performances by the embryonic Van Halen was witnessed by soon-to-be band member and bass player Michael Anthony, who wasn't sure he liked everything he saw. While impressed by the guitar player and the drummer, the singer, in particular, seemed to Anthony to have something indefinably unsettling about him. Roth, he recalled later, was prancing around on stage as if he owned the place, and sporting too much of a theatrical get-up for his tastes – he was wearing 'some kind of a tux vest with a cane and a hat . . .'

> He had long hair. I don't know if he had it colored, but I know he had done something weird to it. And he said [to me], 'How do you like my boys?' And I just went, 'Jesus Christ, get this guy away from me.'[33]

But, despite such initial reservations, Anthony leapt at the opportunity to join the band and be corrupted by such showbiz ways. He ditched his plans to study for a degree in music at the University of Southern California, which got him thrown out of the family home. But he was soon rehearsing with Roth and the Van Halens at the crumbling Hanky Hacienda, and would in short measure be treading the boards of the little stages the band erected in suburban Pasadena backyards for the kind of perennial weekend blowouts that seemed to mark the 1970s, in Roth's words, as one big time-out. He played along with Roth's idea of putting on a show and later claimed that on his debut he sported a gold lamé suit – as Elvis Presley had famously done on the cover of the 50,000,000 *Elvis Fans Can't Be Wrong* album – while on the other side of the stage Eddie was reputedly clad in a silver lamé vest and pants.

It is worth pausing to reflect on this use of backyards for purposes unforeseen by their owners as one more detail in California's long-drawn-out affair with the idea of self-invention as the chief goal in life. Unsurprisingly, it had a non-musical cultural parallel elsewhere in Southern California at exactly the same time. As Van Halen invaded the gardens of Pasadena, so – down by the Pacific Ocean in Venice Beach – a gang of surfers with no waves to catch after the sea had gone out for the day decided they would reinvent surfing as skateboarding. Skateboards had already existed, of course, but what the new innovators did was to throw out its dull show-pony 1960s origins and infuse it with a dash of rock'n'roll irreverence. They sought out the curved concrete swimming pools of empty residential properties – drained of water and left to dry out in the long summers – which soon provided something akin to a concrete wave that could be 'surfed' all day.

For Van Halen and others like them, rock'n'roll was played out in the Edenic Southern Californian surrounding of the garden just when it didn't make it to the bars or clubs; when it was the only way they could make their own, very different, waves. They improvised venues in the grounds of family homes, which could often be so large that they were set in several acres of Mediterranean parkland. Roth told the magazine *Wax Paper* in 1978 that these events – where the beer would flow and the celebrations commence early in the afternoon as the band set up its equipment – demanded the trappings of a proper show, because they were drawing big crowds, with numbers said to be upwards of a thousand people who would pay a dollar each for entry.[34]

For that small donation to Van Halen's continued existence the audience witnessed improvised smoke bombs – made with gunpowder that had been pressed into electrically charged cat food cans and attached to a footswitch. These would be set off by bass player Mike Anthony at the end of a particularly energetic number, or when proceedings needed a bit of livening up – just to ensure the audience were getting it. The stage lights that would come on as the sun began to set had been liberated from their more conventional uses, too: snatched from the grounds of some of Pasadena's finest public buildings and residential gardens, where they were meant to illuminate plants and signs. The size of these events on their own were proof that the band was progressing and, perhaps, outgrowing Pasadena – and by 1976 they would be filling out the 3,000-seat Pasadena Civic Auditorium. Yet, at the same time, beyond San Bernardino County, they were barely known.

They exited the infamous Hanky Hacienda after band-leader Snotty Scotty's brother came home and shut off the electricity during a Van Halen band rehearsal. Eddie got his revenge, Scotty later said, by 'using his '67 Volvo to plough up the vegetable garden' that had been, until then, 'carefully tended by the Hankies' bass player'.[35] It was a sign that they were moving on to pastures new. The distance between Pasadena and Hollywood's Sunset Strip was only, by Roth's calculations, the duration of a side of a cassette tape as one drove westwards along the Hollywood Freeway – about thirteen miles.

'Van Halen – more energy than an atomic reactor', ran the Warner Bros ads.
Van Halen (1978) album sleeve.

4 HANGING TEN, *c.* 1977–82

Only to fury lifted of all horns
Mourning to themselves a thing to come,
For we have seen delirium in a claxon,
Seen revelation lit on chrome.[1]

– Hildegarde Flanner, 'Noon on Alameda Street'

From Pasadena, the Hollywood Freeway brought with it both
the means of Van Halen's arrival and its most unusual instrument.
The first few seconds of *Van Halen* (1978) seem to catch the sound
of the moment the band members rolled into their destination,
horns ablaze, as if to clear the path into their future. Just as soon
as you begin to wonder if it was the sound of some kind of air
raid siren, it is gone. As it fades, its hold on the attention is replaced
by something more earthy and primeval; something that has
crawled out of the swamp. It makes a sound that reverberates
through the body:

> duhr, duhr, duhr,
> duhr, duhr, duhr,
> duhr

After ten seconds or so, there follows a crash and a thud, and Van
Halen burst, fully formed, into existence.

Eddie Van Halen rode the '67 Volvo that had redesigned
the Pasadena garden of Snotty Scotty right into the studio, in a
manner of speaking. There, in the aptly named Sunset Sound
Recorders – formerly a car repair garage – they sacrificed the
'claxons', or horns, that were ripped from their beat-up old cars
(sturdy European Volvos, Opels and Volkswagens) which had, in
a sense, carried them through the previous half decade to this

point. We might read such an act as the fulfilment of the Pasadena poet Hildegarde Flanner's vision of a bucolic arcadia overcome by machine technology. Just like revving engines caught in traffic, ablaze under the sun, Van Halen *sounded* like – even *looked* like – 'loaded radiance that might explode'.[2] Just look at the cover of *Van Halen* and you see it. They are on fire, trailing vapour like some kind of superheroes – Mike Anthony leaks something green and toxic looking, perhaps it was kryptonite. Whatever it was that had been done to 'touch up' the photography, it was done in order to capture the sense of the expenditure of energy – and, as David Lee Roth once said, 'if the music explodes, then so should we.'

Along with the 'duhr' of that swampy electric bass guitar, which morphs into an industrial-sounding metronome (millions of years of history in seven notes), the jet-like blare of those redeployed car horns was a sound that would blast them out into the world beyond California, whose borders they had never crossed as a band.

The prospect onto the future was opened, in a sense, by Van Halen's Fowley and Bingenheimer connection. Following a series of events that those two had instigated – not least Van Halen playing The Starwood and The Whisky A Go Go – the president of Warner Bros Records, Mo Ostin and producer Ted Templeman were invited to The Starwood to see the band in the autumn of 1977. Once there, Templeman knew right away that he would sign the band: 'Five steps in the door I was hit with the lightning bolt', he said later. 'The guitar player. I knew this was it. The third of the greats. Parker, Tatum and this guy.'[3] 'This guy' – Eddie – Templeman would compare, on several occasions, to Charlie Parker:

> Eddie Van Halen is the most amazing musician I've ever been around. He's like Charlie Parker, man – he's a monster. He can do things with a guitar that other people just can't do.[4]

It is an unusual and remarkable comparison. It would surely be an accolade for any guitar player who had spent the last six years playing bars, wet T-shirt contests and beer parties. Charlie Parker, more than just a sax player, was an innovator whose music could not be contrived. As W. T. Lhamon said, this music of Parker's was about 'speed and nimble chaos, the sound of someone extraordinarily attentive to the present moment' who couldn't help but break the limitations others had imposed on jazz.[5] And it was that kind of quality that perhaps Templeman had in mind – this tendency not only to ignore the rules, but also an almost total obliviousness to where it came from, this mysterious talent. In other respects, too, as I suggest later, Eddie's playing was often more akin – in spirit and phrasing – to bebop. Without Templeman's encouragement, though, and without sound engineer Donn Landee's way with helping guitarists to realize the tones and textures they had in mind, it is difficult to imagine that Van Halen could have achieved such a spectacular, explosive arrival.

Templeman and Landee would steer Van Halen through the making of their first album and be on hand to produce their next five. They brought out Van Halen's capacity for unthinking, spontaneous creation in a body of work recorded between 1977 and 1983 that was made in something of the order of two to three months total studio time. During demo sessions for Warners in 1977 the band quickly gave Templeman the idea of how they would be recorded. According to Landee, they 'cut 28 songs in about two hours', laying tracks down much as if they were giving a stage performance. It was a testament to almost five years of solid gigging around Southern California, which amounted to perhaps hundreds of live shows. These demo sessions served mainly to document the band's original material, which allowed Templeman to think about the shape and content of their first album. Although the band had been signed on the basis of their live show, it wasn't until they were in the studio that the record company really knew what they had – after a couple of hours in the studio, Landee said, 'we knew we had a band who could play'.[6]

Many of the first songs that the band recorded, however, were not considered as being up to scratch. One song that never made the cut was 'Young and Wild', co-authored by Kim Fowley. It was a song that bore superficial similarities to the kind of tunes Fowley had co-written with KISS – 'Do You Love Me' and 'King of the Nighttime World', on their album of 1976, *Destroyer* – but with none of the verve or glam pop elan of those songs. Fragments and riffs from other songs recorded in these early sessions remained in a bag of cassette tapes that Eddie would carry around on the road over the years to come: works in progress. Many would appear over the next five years transformed, often with the addition of better vocal lines and lyrics, but with musical sections that were often more or less intact.

Throughout late 1977 Van Halen continued gigging on the Strip. When the time came to begin sessions for the album proper they moved to the famed Sunset Sound Recorders, a studio built in the 1950s by the Walt Disney producer 'Tutti' Camarata. At one time the studio functioned 'almost as an extension of the Disney lot', with 'soundtracks recorded, edited and mixed there'.[7] The studio also had its own mastering equipment, allowing discs to be cut on site. Since the earliest days of its existence the studio's unique sonic qualities were put down not only to the physical characteristics of the actual space (being an ex-garage, its sloping concrete floor had been designed to let engine oil and the like run into a gutter – something that is also good for creating a live sound), but also to the various sound engineers and producers who found ways to utilize the peculiarities that distinguished it from other local studios. In the case of Van Halen, Templeman and Landee decided to make use of the studio's characteristic 'natural' sound – a property of its unique reverberation sound field – and opted for minimal overdubs and a live feel.

This approach employed room ambience and, in particular, the way that instruments – guitars, bass and drums – would bleed into the microphones set up to capture individual tracks. By the 1970s, it is useful to recall, it had become common to aim for a drier sound where instrumental and vocal tracks were kept separate – even if it was due just to baffles and separators in the studio that were placed between a group of musicians who played at the same time. The Ted Templeman approach for Van Halen was to leave the instrument bleeds in to accurately represent the sound of the band playing live as a unit. It had another purpose insofar as the production team believed in going with early takes, and wanted to capture the band's sound 'before they really knew what they were doing – just have them come in and play and then get them out'.[8] One quality that characterizes the album is that the tunes, for the most part, don't come to a neat ending or fade gradually. They tend to end with a bang or a crash, a final flash of energy, just as they would do onstage.

Within such a set-up there were serendipitous moments and unexpected departures from the norm. A good example of Templeman and Landee's ability to help the band produce something that might have otherwise never seen the light of day is to be found in 'Eruption'. It was a piece recorded, by all accounts, as an absolute fluke – 'a total freak occurrence' in Eddie's words, when he and Alex Van Halen were warming up in the studio before one of their last shows at The Whisky A Go Go on the Sunset Strip.[9] Templeman and Landee had left the tape rolling without saying anything to the brothers, and what would become known as 'Eruption' – a couple of minutes of guitar artistry that would soon enough see Eddie declared the new Hendrix – was merely a backstage warm-up that allowed Eddie to stretch and loosen his fingers. The producer sat in the control room hearing it for the first time, which seems remarkable given what it would do in underlining Van Halen's arrival.

Crowds gather on Sunset Strip for what would be Van Halen's penultimate show at The Whisky A Go Go on 31 December 1977. It is thought to have been earlier this evening that Eddie and Alex Van Halen 'accidentally' cut the landmark instrumental 'Eruption' during a warm-up at Sunset Sound studios.

What appears on record as a result is the one and only 'take', after a couple of times running through it. On hearing this explosive, souped-up, baroque hot-rod of a tune – punctuated by the sound of dive-bombs, groans and barely comprehensible squeals in between passages that soar effortlessly as if they had found a pathway onto the jet stream – Templeman knew in an instant that it had to go on the album, and it had to be right up front in the listener's face. This wasn't another filler instrumental designed to kill a spare minute or two, but something that he was sure no one would have heard the likes of before. As the musicologist Robert Walser notes, 'Eruption' was

> one minute and twenty-seven seconds of exuberant and playful virtuosity, a violinist's precise and showy technique inflected by the vocal rhetoric of the blues and rock and roll reverence. Here . . . Van Halen's guitar playing displays an unprecedented fluidity.[10]

From this 87-second accident, Eddie suddenly found people like Frank Zappa – a man who preferred to express himself at rather greater length on guitar – thanking him in the press for 'reinventing' the guitar. More than 30 years later 'Eruption', despite the hundreds of bad adaptations by imitators, still sounds astonishing and unmatchable in terms of its energy and attack – has the capacity to take the listener right back to that moment, arguably, because it was never intended to be immortalized in this fashion.

However, it was because of 'Eruption' that Eddie came to be regarded in many quarters as a tricksy, showy player – those later approximations and crude homages it gave birth to preceded the original. For Eddie, the technique displayed on 'Eruption' wasn't contrived or forced – it was just what it was: a kind of breathing or relaxing into the music; a letting go that had more in common with the loss of inhibitions one heard, as Ted Templeman might have said, in the playing of Charlie Parker.

One other significant element of Van Halen's sound that Donn Landee was able to translate onto tape was what can best be described as a kind of 'airiness'. 'Ain't Talkin' 'Bout Love' (*Van Halen*), for instance, seems to pitch the listener right into a gust of rising, swirling air. It is a sound that seemed to fit with those bleeding colours, or 'vapour trails', that can be seen coming from the bodies of the band on the cover of *Van Halen*, diffusing them into the atmosphere. Sonically, this spatial quality was partly the result of the sweeping and gusting effect of the cheap MXR flangers Eddie employed on the album. A flanger is, essentially, a means of synthesizing sound – a crude tool for altering and processing an input signal. Eddie's increasing use of synthesizers from about 1980–81 (and particularly on 'Jump', recorded in 1983) is not nearly as much of a departure as it appeared at the time, if we consider the flanger's historical relationship to the synthesizer. In *Electronic and Computer Music* (2004), Peter Manning notes that the flanger was mostly identifiable through 'acoustic interactions in air' that could create 'strange illusions of spatial movement' (phasing and flanging) precisely in the way that listeners became accustomed to keyboard synthesizers doing.[11] All of that, however, might have failed to work its effect without the availability of Sunset Sound's famed echo chamber.

By the 1960s, the studio was a popular choice for Los Angeles bands such as Love and The Doors, with the latter recording a series of albums with long-time Sunset Sound engineer Bruce Botnick behind the console.

Botnick, in fact, has spoken with a sense of wonder at the qualities of the studio's echo chamber – this great reverb room, he said, was all about 'longitude, latitude and zenith'.[12] What he meant by that was that no two echo chambers ever seem to be able to produce the same results, precisely because they cannot occupy the same physical location. In fact, the owners of Sunset Sound once tried to build a replica of the original echo chamber to help service the two original studios in the complex (there are now three studios) and in the design and construction used the same materials and spatial dimensions, but the resulting room never worked as expected. This original Sunset chamber used by The Doors and Van Halen, among others, was constructed as a more or less rectangular room of non-parallel walls – which is to say, the walls and floors were at differing angles in order attain the desired room reverb, which was created by sound bouncing around off the surfaces.

All of this took place on the floor above the performance area of the studio – 'built inside of a block wall', as Botnick said, it was sealed off behind the closure of a meat locker door. Inside it was made of nothing but wood, which was the cladding on top of layers and layers of drywall, with 'maybe about twenty or thirty coats of resin over it . . .'

> So it felt like a wooden room. You could go in there, sit down and turn the light off and think you were in the biggest wooden room you've ever been in.[13]

In fact, the room was very small and only a few feet wide. The source sound that would be subjected to reverb was fed out of the main studio and through a large speaker that was situated at one end of the small room of the echo chamber. The echo from the room was then captured by a microphone set up at the opposite end from this speaker, catching the live sound created by Eddie's guitar back in the studio as it was being modified by this unique sonic space. Its effect can be heard on The Doors' 'Light My Fire', the crack of the opening snare, and the bossa nova rimshots of drummer John Densmore and the guitar of Robby Krieger at the beginning of 'Break On Through'.[14] On the *Van Halen* album – especially given the lack of overdubbing that resulted from recording as a band – the echo was used to add depth to the studio performance and further enhanced the sound Eddie had developed as a result of his own fairly elaborate guitar and amplifier modifications. In addition to what the studio added in reverb, he employed an old tape echo device that was housed in the casing of a huge Second World War practice bomb. Curious audience members at Van Halen's early shows would spot this mysterious-looking object onstage, standing almost 3 metres (10 feet) tall next to his speaker cabinets. Rather than functioning in a manner that might live up to Roth's frequent declaration that of 'if the music explodes, so must we', it would contribute modest effects such as those heard in the throbbing, dying seconds of 'Eruption'.

The simplicity of *Van Halen* derived from the fact that, as Templeman later said, all he had to do to get a take was to gather the band members in the studio and 'put a microphone in front of them'.[15] The album's stereo 'picture' is extremely uncluttered and basic, with song performances for the most part consisting of just three instruments – guitar, bass and drums – and the vocals of Roth (and the rest of the band on backgrounds and harmony). Otherwise, the album deftly conveys a sense of space, perhaps as close as it is possible to conjure up the sense of being in the room when it was being performed. Just how basic the set-up was can be illustrated by the fact that if Landee and Templeman hadn't panned Eddie's guitar to one side of the stereo picture (they used the echo from it to occupy space on the other) and had instead put it squarely in the middle, they might have wound up, as Landee said later, 'with the whole band in mono'.[16]

Even by the standards of the 'back to basics' punk ethos of the time – 1977 – Van Halen were recording fairly primitively, although very professionally, and using a sixteen-track console quite sparingly with lots of 'room left over' after all the tracks and vocals had been recorded.[17] Even the Sex Pistols' Steve Jones – to cite a contemporaneous example of punk's supposed back-to-basics approach – layered dozens of identical guitar tracks on *Never Mind the Bollocks* to achieve a distinctive fat slab of a sound. On *Van Halen* one single guitar track (and the echo, of course) produces an explosive effect. But, as Templeman recalled, it was mainly the result of Eddie's ability to produce the goods in single takes:

Almost every solo you hear is played live on the basic track. He'll whip into the solo, then go right back into the verse. When you've got that kind of musicianship, you don't have to do much work.[18]

If it sounded slick, it was the result of the band having played many hundreds of shows. Clearly, and despite the Sunset Strip associations, Van Halen weren't a punk band. 'Ain't Talkin' 'Bout Love' was Eddie's version of a throwaway two-chord punk song – yet in common with the punk bands they went for immediacy

Van Halen pictured at Venice Beach, Los Angeles, early 1978. Left to right: David Lee Roth, Michael Anthony, Alex and Eddie Van Halen.

and short punchy tunes, rather than over-elaboration and the meandering epics born of the Prog Rock era of the 1970s. And, as with punk, it was almost as if the bloated and over-indulgent early years of that decade had never happened. This was a factor that made Van Halen very cheap to record (and thus highly profitable to Warner Bros once the albums started going platinum) in an era of rising costs. Van Halen's budget of about $50,000 dollars, the *Los Angeles Times* reported in a story exploring soaring studio budgets, was up to ten times less than the budget for some albums of the time, such as Bruce Springsteen's *Darkness on the Edge of Town* (1978) and Fleetwood Mac's *Rumours* (1977).[19]

By 1977 Templeman and Landee had worked together for most of the decade on the albums of a number of Warner and Reprise artists – these included the likes of Van Morrison, Captain Beefheart, Little Feat and the Doobie Brothers. Landee had even worked as a studio engineer on some of Templeman's last recordings with Harpers Bizarre, the band he sang and played drums for in the mid- to late 1960s before he ended up working at Warner Bros Records. They formed a successful working unit and delivered a series of albums that aimed to live up to Warner Bros' repu-tation as the best record company on the West Coast.[20] But Templeman's role in Van Halen's career was more than that of hired hand.

The 1970s may have coincided with the last years of an era in which record companies truly had the ability to mould a roster of artists according to some kind of aesthetic (or, at worst, corporate) ideal. This was something that was due largely to the influence of the Artist and Repertoire (or 'A&R') executive. As it happened, Templeman was Van Halen's A&R – as well as their producer – which meant not only that he held an executive position within the record company but also a directing influence on the band's musical direction. It extended in particular to their choice of material and – especially in their early days – to their development as songwriters. The point of all this, of course, was that the A&R arm of a company was intended to ensure a measure of quality control over creative output.[21]

The standard alternative working model – far more common today following the relative decline of record companies as entities with a distinctive identity or ethos – was for a producer to go independent and take a cut of the artist's gross earnings on a record. Templeman, though, was happy enough with a situation that saw him principally as the representative of the company in the studio and he once said that he'd 'take a pay cut rather than work anywhere other than Warner Reprise'.[22] His influence on the recorded output of Van Halen, in the end, derived less from a signature sound than from the way he ran the sessions and the ambience he created towards delivering good takes, as well as making decisions over what takes would be used – a very important criterion in blocking the tendency of musicians to beat the life out of a song through repeated takes.

When we look at photographs of Ted on the Harpers Bizarre albums we see what might be the stereotypical Californian – sun-bleached hair, and looking like an extra from the cult surf movie *Big Wednesday*. Some weight was given to such an impression when he told one interviewer that he'd have been happy to spend his days surfing if he hadn't been rescued by Warner Bros after the demise of the odd entity that was Harpers Bizarre.[23] They were a 1960s vocal harmony group that Joseph Lanza, in his book *Vanilla Pop* (2005), suggests were defined by the 'pillowy graces' of their baroque choirboy harmonies. As a singer, Lanza notes, Templeman was no macho frontman but, on the contrary, had been noted for a distinctive 'feminine tone'.[24]

Much of the Harpers' material consisted of cover tunes – their biggest hit being a version of Simon and Garfunkel's '59th Street Bridge Song (Feeling Groovy)'. Traversing the era

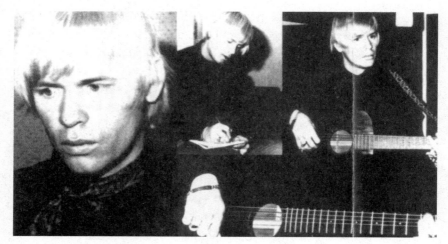

Ted Templeman pictured on the sleeve of his final album with Harpers Bizarre, *Harpers Bizarre 4* (1969).

of mid-1960s guitar rock and late 1960s psychedelia, they seem a quaint oddity today – but there were some gems among their output – sublime moments such as 'Witchi Tai To', a song that appeared on *Harpers Bizarre 4* (1969). In the sleeve notes to this – their final album – Templeman's fellow band member (and brother-in-law) John Petersen observed that the future vice-president of Warner Bros Records was 'a gentle person'; a man of taste and refinement, no less, 'an admirer of Spanish archi-tecture and fine racing machines'. Yet the meagre details of Templeman's biography, gleaned from traces left in a few inter-views, don't hint that he could be a bit of a dictator in the studio.

When Templeman joined Warner Bros in 1970 he became part of one of the most respected and prestigious record companies around. They were then developing an A&R and staff production team whose task was to establish the label as both the shrewdest and the coolest in the business – and as a result their early 1970s A&R department sought to cover a wide spectrum of rock and pop music.[25] Alongside Templeman Warners hired producers Russ

Warners' Newest

Super Group:

Waronker, Wickham, Templeman, Titleman & Cale

In this business, cities have sounds. New Orleans and Kansas City got known for Dixieland sounds. Memphis has its, and so does Detroit. Nashville, too.

And incredibly, there's

The Burbank Sound

It's the responsibility of Lenny Waronker.

He is leader of Warners' A&R staff, the company's latest supergroup.

The Burbank Sound may be his responsibility, but if you were to ask Mr. Waronker what the Burbank Sound is, he'd say he never heard of it.

Other people, of course, have: among them Captain Beefheart, John Cale, Ry Cooder, The Doobie Brothers, Arlo Guthrie, Gordon Lightfoot, Little Feat, Van Morrison, Randy Newman, Van Dyke Parks, Ed Sanders, for sure.

Each of these artists has recorded with a producer from the ranks of Warner's new supergroup—with Lenny Waronker, Andy Wickham, Ted Templeman, Russ Titleman or John Cale—the five pictured above.

Good Men.

(Ted Templeman, for instance, has most recently watched his latest Burbank Sound single—"Listen to the Music," by the Doobie Brothers—capture America.)

Sweated Subtleties

The Burbank Sound is, in essence, the result of a drive—often near interminable—toward perfection.

The drive to get a single or album recorded plumperfect. To redo and redo a record, even to the point where producer and artist spend hours sweating over subtleties that might well go unheard on the final record.

That sweating costs money and spirits, but it earns a Sound with capital S.

Earlier in '72, for example, Lenny's artist Arlo Guthrie had been long overdue for an album. The merchandising guys at the other end of the humble Warner/Reprise building were a-gnash. They bitched about "losing momentum" (as they put it) because "Arlo's been off the market so long."

And Lenny would listen and nod gravely, and he would say yes that certainly is so and what a shame but Arlo just hasn't felt like it 'til recently, fellas.

Mirabile dictu, that settled the matter.

When Arlo did, however, feel like recording some more, the Burbank Sound and the Burbank Supergroup were available. Month after month, available, until Mr. Guthrie and Lenny knew it could be no better.

And at that time only did Lenny Waronker slip the album to Warners by-then rather randy sales boys.

Out of that album smashed Arlo's *City of New Orleans.*

History should note: the City of New Orleans owes a lot to Burbank, and Burbank's Sound.

Thank you Arlo, but thank you Supergroup, too.

That Supergroup is why the Burbank Sound sounds better and better.

Even if it takes longer.

Even if it costs more.

Supergroups like Waronker, Wickham, Templeman, Titleman, and Cale happen neither cheap nor hasty.

But they happen in Burbank.

Where they belong.

An advert from the music trade publication, *Billboard* (October 1972).

Titelman, Andy Wickham and John Cale, co-founder of avant-garde rock innovators The Velvet Underground. Cale would go on to produce two obscure albums with Templeman during his time at Warner Bros for an act that went by the name of Chunky, Novi and Ernie. In his memoir, *What's Welsh for Zen*, Cale recalled the atmosphere at Warners Bros' Burbank HQ as being something like a teachers' common room, into which various musicians and managers – their erstwhile 'students' within this A&R setup – would drop in to talk about sessions and promotional matters.[26]

There was more to Ted, however, than the mellow-dude-with-surfer-aspirations impression suggests. He was, as it happens, a hardened survivor of encounters with difficult performers – Van Morrison, in particular. When he began working with Morrison, for instance, he was still relatively inexperienced and unsure of his role in the studio. The Belfast-born singer, on the other hand, was already a fairly well-established figure, generally accepted to be possessed of a singular artistic vision as well as having a bruising reputation as a no-nonsense performer. Morrison's landmark album, *Astral Weeks* (1968), was then seen as – and remains to this day – one of the high-water marks of rock music. But Templeman was perceived by Morrison – not incorrectly – as the record company's inside man, potentially out to thwart his artistic ambitions on the album *Tupelo Honey* (1971), the first they made together. Inevitably the two had divergent ideas about how the album should sound, and Morrison departed the sessions saying he never wanted Templeman, who got the final say over the mixes, near his music again. Ted, for his part, declared that he had 'aged ten years' working with Morrison. Despite the singer's evident genius, he mused that nothing could bring the two of them back into the same studio – 'even if he offered me $3 million in cash'. 'He's fired everyone who has ever worked with him: all his producers, his managers, his attorneys, his wife, his kids.'[27]

But, of course, as events transpired they did work together again – on *St Dominic's Preview* (1972) and *It's Too Late to Stop Now* (1974), an album that was long held to be one of the best live albums ever released. However, in the early days, one advantage Templeman had with Van Halen over other more established artists he had produced was that he more or less plucked them from nowhere, giving them their first proper chance in a studio with the full weight of a record company's backing and the freedom not to have to feel they were being auditioned.

The band also wanted him as a producer, and were over the moon when he personally signed them to Warner Bros – mainly because they were big fans of two albums he had made with San Francisco-based hard-rock band Montrose – *Montrose* (1973) and *Paper Money* (1974). This was the band formed, as it happened, by Van Morrison's guitarist on two of the three albums Templeman had produced, Ronnie Montrose, and a bass player named Bill Church who had also played on Morrison's *Tupelo Honey*. But Montrose – most notably in the story of Van Halen – also featured the singer then billed as 'Sam Hagar' who, by mid-1985, would find himself in Van Halen.

In many regards Van Halen were a throwback to an earlier era when bands that functioned as regular performing units recorded live and, essentially, as a unit. This wasn't The Beatles (or acts who followed in their wake) retreating to the studio to experiment. Rather than mucking around writing songs in the studio (although the occasional song was made this way), as many bands by the mid-1970s had become accustomed to doing, Van Halen worked up their new material on the road and in the basement of the Roth family house in Pasadena. 'We invite Ted down [to rehearsals], and he picks what he likes', Eddie told one interviewer in 1980. 'We argue a bit, compromise, and we [the band] usually have a final say on which material gets recorded.'[28] By the time Van Halen entered the studio – and this was largely true for the first five albums at least – the major part of Templeman's job was to get a sound, make sure the atmosphere was right and set the tapes rolling. Once, when Roth couldn't quite get the take that Templeman wanted – something in his voice didn't seem right – he was sent out with orders to eat a greasy burger, drink some beer and smoke a joint.

With Templeman always keen to spend as little time in the studio as possible, a devil-may-care attitude prevailed. This allowed the pressure of any particular day – or the dynamics of any given situation in the studio – to throw up whatever it might; to allow, so to speak, the 'creative unconscious' to make its own contribution. It was then, Roth said, that 'you've got something that really explodes, that's spontaneous, that *ignites*':

> You're under pressure; the people are putting pressure on you in the studio: you're paying money and you don't have the words just right or the music isn't just right. And if all that pressure is there you're gonna have something that just goes KABOOM! It might go kaboom really badly but, it's like, wow – where'd *that* come from!?[29]

It all worked, the singer believed, because Van Halen were constantly 'on maximum': 'Sometimes it's a battle to keep us from turning everything up into the red zone – the needle isn't supposed to go into the red – but that's where Van Halen live.'[30]

The result was a sense of spontaneity that suggested the songs were knocked out live, in a single shot, which was largely the case. Reviewing *Van Halen II* (1979), *Rolling Stone*'s Timothy White suggested that the album's chief characteristic was a 'numbing live feel'. Roth, he noted, battled it out with Eddie for the listener's attention with a 'repertoire of deft UH-HUHS and train-whistle exhortations', which White transcribed for his readers ('WHOA-HHAO WHOOOOOOOOO!'). In parts, the record had a distinctive *vérité* feel to it as the vocals segued 'into snickers . . . shared by the entire group'.[31] In an era characterized by overproduction, and when even 'live albums were taken back to the studio for cleaning and fixing up, Van Halen aimed for a sound that was as real as possible. 'Dig it or not', White concluded in his *Rolling Stone* review,

> I've had this amazing thirty-one-minute artefact on my
> turntable for hours, and after almost one careful listening
> I'm utterly convinced that the members of Van Halen must
> have been up half the night creating it. What an effort.[32]

Undoubtedly, the match-up of Templeman and Van Halen
worked because the band's work ethic never forced him to resort
to the kind of tactics – he once said he had 'a Nazi way of running
things' – required for artists who were more leisurely in their
approach to recording.[33] Once, when working with Little Feat,
Templeman was having trouble getting through to the band's
gifted but temperamental singer and guitarist, Lowell George
(who didn't take too kindly to a bit of criticism from Templeman
during a session and then refused to show up at the studio the
next morning to re-cut a solo as he was supposed to). Ted didn't
like to indulge the tantrums that musicians would throw, so he
just called the next best slide guitar player he knew in Los Angeles
– Bonnie Raitt – to finish the record off for him. 'She came down
and played a fuckin' killer solo', he later recalled. But crucially,
in this game of who's the boss, Templeman intended all along
for Lowell George to know about it, and played Bonnie Raitt's
take over the phone to goad the Little Feat guitarist into action:
'I called Lowell and I said, "listen to this. What do you think?
Doesn't this burn?"' The guitarist was so out of his mind with
rage at being replaced on his own record that he was soon at the
studio – still dressed in his pyjamas – determined to outdo Bonnie
Raitt's effort.[34]

But, with Van Halen, things went smoothly for a long time:
Van Halen II was finished in a week, just two days after the band had
completed a tour that had seen them on the road for eight months
– they cut four songs in one day. It would be the same for *Women
and Children First* (1978) – four days on the music and another four
days a week later, after a break, working on the vocals. And *Diver*

Down (1982) was recorded in six days for less than it cost to cut their first album in 1977.[35]

By 1981, however, Eddie was dreaming of the kind of control someone like The Beach Boys' Brian Wilson had had in his heyday – spending six months on one song was nothing for Wilson. With the help of Landee, he found himself sneaking into Sunset Sound during the recording of *Fair Warning* (1981) when Templeman and the rest of band were not around to put down the parts Templeman wanted in the way he heard them.

5 HOLLYWOOD FLOTSAM, c. 1980–82

It's like a bowl of granola round here. Whatever isn't fruit and nuts is flakes, man.

— David Lee Roth in Hollywood, 1981

In *Repo Man*, a film set in the early 1980s, the hero Otto Maddox, played by Emilio Estevez, cruises Los Angeles reclaiming cars under the guidance of a shifty character named Bud (played by Harry Dean Stanton) who sees the repo business as something akin to social hygiene. 'Look at 'em', he says, pointing from the window of a sedan as they cruise the streets of the Los Angeles that the tourists never see. 'Ordinary fucking people, I hate 'em.' Los Angeles – once described by Reyner Banham as 'Autopia' – was the perfect setting for a movie that played on the centrality of the car to daily life. But it was more than that.

Otto – whose name is itself a play on 'Auto' – is an unemployable misfit who suddenly finds himself, accidentally, in an occupation where he can distinguish himself as one of the best. Taking cars from under the noses of unsuspecting owners comes naturally to him, it's just like stealing without the risks – a jape, a daily adventure filled with cackling laughter directed at the ordinary suckers unlucky enough to have fallen behind in their loan repayments. What made it such a perfect job was just that its informal and undercover workings seemed to be in tune with something else rumbling under the surface of the Los Angeles – the Hollywood – that presented itself to the world. The fictional Otto, that is to say, had found a home amid the contemporary Los Angeles underground, the alternative and hardcore music scene, which sprouted like a stubborn weed all over Hollywood at the turn of the 1980s. This, of course, was much to the annoyance of those who – as in previous eras – preferred a bit of order in the garden. *Repo Man* and its soundtrack – featuring Los Angeles bands of the era, such as Circle Jerks, Black Flag and The Plugz – would also form the soundtrack and background to David Lee Roth's life in Hollywood during the years 1980–82, and inspire his odd, unusual, celebration of those years – Van Halen's 'Top Jimmy', released on their *MCMLXXXIV/1984* album.

The song offered one of the rare occasions when Roth's lyrics weren't just channelling a sense of exuberance, but instead seemed to have some conventional biographical and factual content. The individual who went by the name of Top Jimmy – unknown to anyone outside Hollywood's underground bars and clubs – was for real, a hero of the demimonde of *Repo Man*. The song named after him recounted a night in 1981 at a seedy Los Angeles club, when he and his band, The Rhythm Pigs, 'brought the roof down' during a raucous set of beer-soaked R'N'B. But the story of the song that would become 'Top Jimmy', once Roth had added the words to an already-existing piece of music by Eddie (that in tone and texture sounded quite unlike anything that might exemplify the idea of hard rock), takes us further than the events of a singular evening. Set to a soundtrack seemingly composed of a warped surf instrumental and a vocal by Roth and Mike Anthony that seems infinitely more Devo than Dio, it celebrates all that Top Jimmy represented in Los Angeles – the authenticity of the real, living, breathing, rock'n'roll that just kept on going beneath the cheap glitz of Hollywood. It was music that lived, for a time, in the basements of cheap restaurants and dingy bars, unsullied by the compromises of the Los Angeles music business.

By early 1980, just two years after Van Halen's last shows at The Whisky, the Los Angeles club scene saw the emergence of a new breed of fast and raw bands that broke into Hollywood from neighbouring counties and outlying suburbs. For many they were considered to be representative of an entirely new breed of outright violent teenagers, inspired by the 'up yours' attitude of punk – they came from places like Orange County and Hermosa Beach, home to disaffected surf punks. Don Waller, who at the time ran a fanzine called *Back Door Man*, recalled that the clubs and bars of the Strip and beyond soon filled up with 'psychotic teenage runaways', whose outer fringes – and their favoured bands – would be documented in Penelope Spheeris's acclaimed film about it all, *The Decline of Western Civilization* (1981).

In some ways these developments harked back to the more thriving Hollywood club scene of the mid-1960s. But, as the English journalist Mick Farren noted, the new musical culture faced as much opposition as any that had gone before because ' the surf punks wrecked every place that allowed them to play'.[1] The response of the authorities to this enlivened youth culture seemed to be a repeat of the events of 1966 – which is to say, what followed was a heavy-handed police clampdown on the alternative underground. Farren's long article on the scene for *New Musical Express* (*NME*) in early 1981 reported that, contrary to expectations, sightings of the apparently menacing punks were very rare – they seemed, in fact, to be almost non-existent. He wondered what all the fuss was about until he realized that they were mostly in hiding – from the Los Angeles Police Department. It was *they* who were highly visible, partly to keep the streets clear of undesirables. As Farren reported, the police could be seen, 'riding around in shining Harley Davidson Electraglides in gangs of ten or a dozen, looking like highly groomed Hell's Angels'.[2] When he did make contact with the scene, however, it was clear that this was a different strain of punk than the phenomenon that hit the UK during 1976–7. It seemed, in fact, distinctively more Californian – hedonistic, non-political – and apparently concerned with no more than riding the wave of its ongoing moment. 'These

Angelino kids have no truck with The Clash's chic third world liberation fantasies', Farren noted. Why? The answer was that they were more often set on oblivion: 'fuelled on speed, barbiturates and beer, they use irrational fist-swinging aggression as their only emotional outlet'.[3]

Back in 1977, a Scot who had relocated to Los Angeles, Brendan Mullen, had opened the first dedicated punk club in the city, named The Masque. But, by 1980, he had seen the growth of violence attached to the new scene as a sure sign that it was all but washed-up. 'The newly arrived suburban hardcore scene had become the almost exclusive domain of confused post-adolescent boys suffering from Displaced Testosterone Syndrome' he later wrote.[4] Worse still, any non-aggressive presence that might have found some breathing room amid the violent outbursts was gradually scared away. Mullen noted sagely that 'female attendance plummeted' in the clubs, a sure sign of its doomed future: 'what girls wanted to partake in this idiotic mess?'[5]

However, there were a small number of people – or, in the eyes of these new punks, wimps who 'flopped the hardcore testo rage rite'[6] – who didn't want to play the game and turned their backs on the violent elements of the scene. They began to look elsewhere – to new bands and emerging clubs that put on a kind of roots-rock music that had also begun to emerge in Los Angeles in the 1980s. These bands, playing rock'n'roll, hard-driving R'n'B and cowpunk, were part of a series of seemingly endless mini-scenes that would sprout around various locales, finding a home in some new venue, only to disappear in short order. However, while what was going on musically was often short-lived – fireworks that lit up the sky with brief, captivating flourishes – the roots-rock scene did produce more durable acts, such as Los Lobos (the Chicano band from East Los Angeles) and The Blasters (from Pasadena) who, along with bands like X (a part of the pre-hardcore punk scene), began to carve out a niche for themselves in this alternative Hollywood. One other band that moved around this scene was Top Jimmy and the Rhythm Pigs, a guitar- and sax-driven R'N'B act. 'Jimmy', according to writer and witness to it all, Don Snowden, 'sounded more like Howlin' Wolf than any big ole drunken white boy from Kentucky had any right to'.[7]

Top Jimmy had acquired his nickname as a result of working at Top Taco, a fast food stand across the road from the A&M Records lot on La Brea Avenue. Like many aspiring performers, his real name – James Koncek – didn't have the same showbiz potential as his stage name. For a couple of years before he found The Rhythm Pigs he would play with pick-up bands and, in the spirit of the time and place, get his set together on the day of a show. The main aim was usually to have a good time and get drunk, and so the band of shifting musicians took a name that reflected this attitude – 'Top Jimmy and the All-Drunk All-Stars', no matter who eventually ended up on stage. None of them were really stars – unless you counted the likes of Ray Manzarek of The Doors or Exene Cervenka of X, who would sometimes take the stage as guests. They were, however, always drunk.[8]

When Roth met Top Jimmy it was at the newly opened Zero-Zero club in North Hollywood, in early 1980, where the sometime bluesman was tending bar. This was just as Van Halen were preparing for the release of perhaps their loosest, most underrated album, *Women and Children First* (1980), which, perhaps coincidentally, seemed to be in its own way in tune with a rawer, more vicious kind of attitude. It was an album described variously as sounding like 'ambulances and emergency wards and teeth meeting pavement' and as being 'more ragged than the knees of Joey Ramone's jeans'.[9]

The Zero-Zero was where some of the best-known figures on the Los Angeles alternative and underground scene could be found (alongside notorious party animals like John Belushi, star of films such as *Animal House* and *The Blues Brothers*, and soon to

A newspaper advert for
Van Halen's third
album, *Women and
Children First*, 1980.

be found dead at the Sunset Marquis hotel in Hollywood due
to one night too many of excessive partying). The club, which
would become known as the scene of 'infamous drug orgies and
debauched carousing', was opened in a decrepit boarded-up shop
at 1955 Cahuenga Boulevard by an aspiring actor named John
Pochna, along with some well-known local figures, including
Brendan Mullen, the owner of The Masque.[10] The purpose of
the Zero-Zero was to be simply a place where people could go
and hang out after everywhere else closed at 2 a.m.; partly because
the house parties that people held in the wee small hours were

subject to raids by the police, but mostly because there were too many wired people needing somewhere to party all night.

Pochna stumped up the cash for the venture when it opened at the end of 1980 and figured that the attentions of the police and the licensing authorities could be deflected if they called it an art gallery – but all the while using the space for its intended purpose, which was as a hassle-free gathering place for all the night-birds who didn't want to go to home. Thus, in the words of Mullen, it was really 'an unlicensed after-hours speakeasy . . . masquerading as an art gallery'.[11] Given the ad hoc character of its after-hours existence, it had little more in the way of hospitality than a couple of fridges stocking cold beer, a DJ spinning some records (or, alternatively, there was a jukebox) and a crowd of people who would arrive armed with the goods to keep the night alive – 'smuggled bottles plus whatever joints, pills or powders they had access to'.[12]

The Zero-Zero quickly began to attract, in the words of one regular, Pleasant Gehman, a bohemian crowd made up of 'artists, photographers, actors, models, writers, filmmakers, club bookers, Eurotrash intellectuals, and, of course, musicians'.[13] Roth, according to Pochna, showed up for the first time with two companions who 'completely freaked out when they saw the look of the place and this raw, totally fucked-up downscale crowd'.[14] Roth, however, loved it and stuck around to become something of a fixture in its shabby surroundings, which were outfitted with suitably low-grade furnishings: 'ratty couches, spindly throwaway tables, and mismatched lamps'.[15]

After a while rumours began to circulate locally that the Van Halen singer was an 'investor' in the Zero. But seeing as it was an unlikely venture in which to expect the kind of return that investments usually bring, nobody really knew what the truth was. No one, that is, but the inner circle of four or five people who started the club in the first place.

The truth was that Roth did end up helping to cover the club's losses, keeping it open when it might have otherwise folded: Pochna and his partners had trouble paying the bills from the start – while they would charge entry at $5 a head and give out a membership card to those who paid and entered, it wasn't in any sense a money-making venture and it didn't bring in enough earnings to be self-sustaining. So, Roth became, as Mullen later wrote, 'the anonymous financial benefactor'.[16] We might guess that Roth's desire to remain anonymous was not just to preserve a sense of equality with others who frequented the club, but also to make sure that media attention wasn't drawn to the semi-illegal activities that enlivened the place – although it did get raided. Roth once talked down his financial involvement as little more than posting bail when the Zero was busted by the police.

Like most others who were to be found around the Hollywood music scene at this time, Top Jimmy only had a passing familiarity with Roth through Van Halen, who were – after a couple of platinum albums – now well known. He had seen them perform some three years before at the Golden West Ballroom in the city of Norwalk, California, in March 1977, when Van Halen opened for The Ramones. Early in 1984, after Van Halen's 'Top Jimmy' had alerted the world beyond Hollywood to his existence, Jimmy told the *Los Angeles Times* that he and Roth had been friends ever since they 'got real drunk and sang a bunch of old blues together'.[17] At that time, Top Jimmy and the Rhythm Pigs had a Monday night residency at the Cathay de Grande, which was located at the corner of Selma and Argyle in Hollywood. It was a sweaty and smelly room in the basement of a Chinese restaurant that served dinners upstairs to a mixture of Vietnamese Angelinos and Vietnam vets.[18] And it was here that The Rhythm Pigs developed a reputation as one of the best live bands in Los Angeles at the time, with performers such as Tom Waits and Stevie Ray

A flyer for Top Jimmy and the Rhythm Pigs, December 1981.

Vaughan showing up to join them on those nights that were billed as 'Blue Mondays'.

Most of the other members of this band were, like Jimmy – at 200 pounds-plus – imposing figures. The then burly guitarist Carlos Guitarlos also acted as doorman at the Zero. Together onstage, as Don Snowden says, they delivered a blend of R'N'B meets 1960s garage rock as they

> metamorphosed into a 4/4 pile driver that recalled the Butter-field Blues Band crossed with The Sonics. It was the blues according to Bam Bam, a rude, crude, often lewd, but never loveless mauling that picked you up, slammed you down, and made dancing to the well-worn blues idiom less an option than a physical imperative.[19]

Perhaps in keeping with the spirit of the band's name, if not his Southern rural roots, Jimmy did actually own a real pig – a pet that went by the name of Nadine. A 'real smart pig', he proudly told one interviewer: 'she can turn the faucet on and off if she wants'. And, like a true Rhythm Pig, Nadine liked nothing more than 'to drink beer and waddle around to r'n'b records'.[20] On one occasion the band intended to take Nadine on stage for a show at the Starwood and had her all set up with a special pair of sun-glasses to avoid the dazzle of the stage lights, but unfortunately the owner stepped in at the last minute to prevent the debut of this augmented version of The Rhythm Pigs.

During this period, Roth had an apartment in Shoreham Drive, a few hundred yards from The Whisky A Go Go, and would spend a lot of time in the clubs, where bands like The Blasters, Los Lobos, Black Flag and The Plugz, among others, regularly played. Joe Keithley, lead singer with the Vancouver punk band D.O.A., remembers meeting a 'completely fucking drunk' Roth, accompanied by an 'equally drunk female companion' and Van Halen bass player Mike Anthony, backstage at The Whisky in 1980 when Roth tried to convince him that what they were doing was just the same as Van Halen: 'You just package it differently', he said.[21] But while the Los Angeles hardcore band Minutemen had recorded a sprint-through of Van Halen's 'Ain't Talkin' 'Bout Love', and went so far as to thank them on their *Double Nickels on the Dime* album (1984) for 'writing timeless music', the truth was that for many of the new punk bands Van Halen – probably like almost any band signed to a major label – could only be corporate sellouts'.

After coming off Van Halen's *Fair Warning* tour of 1981, which had ended in late October with a couple of shows with The Rolling Stones in Florida, Roth joined Top Jimmy and the Rhythm Pigs onstage at the Cathay de Grande – the only time he had played

Top Jimmy and the Rhythm Pigs at the Cathay De Grande, May 1981, on one of countless 'Blue Mondays'. David Lee Roth celebrated the night that the low-hung ceiling fell in on the band in the song, 'Top Jimmy' (1983).

onstage with another band since joining Van Halen in 1973. It wasn't this occasion, though, but another one of the regular Rhythm Pigs appearances at the dingy but spacious Cathay, that provided the scenario for the song 'Top Jimmy'.

Being located in a basement, the club not only sat beneath the restaurant upstairs, but also under a 'false' ceiling. The kind that one might find in office buildings, made up of endless square panels – a flimsy shell that anyone who took the notion to could knock out by reaching up and punching something through. A pivotal figure on the scene at the time, Phast Phreddie Patterson (who later wrote pieces on Van Halen in his guise as a journalist) recalled that one night a well-known band of the day, The Plim-souls, had 'raved it up to such a degree that the guitarists com-pletely destroyed the low-drop ceiling over the small stage'.[22] Gary Leonard's photographs from the Cathay de Grande, many of which can be seen in a book about the period titled *Make the Music Go Bang!* (1997), show a patched-together ceiling, barely a foot or two above the heads of the performers and the crowd.[23]

As Roth tells it in 'Top Jimmy', the ceiling above the dance-floor falls in on the crowd, as if the sheer power of the band's propulsive R'N'B had brought it down. It was a moment worthy of commemorating, in the manner of Chuck Berry's 'Johnny B. Goode', Roth told the *Los Angeles Times*; the kind of event that, with a little bit of artistic licence, might unexpectedly transform the everyday into the extraordinary.[24] Thus in 'Top Jimmy' the events of that night are twisted into the realms of the fantastic, as if Jimmy had – through the fact of the ceiling's collapse – been transported to a parallel world.

Driven by an elastic, staggering (as in drunken) guitar part from Eddie (who achieves a wobbly sound by slapping the strings), the song seems always on the verge of crashing down as it is pursued by a catch-me-if-you-can rush on the drums, which are trying to get ahead of the game. The over-the-top nature of the instrumen-tal music is matched by the words, through which Roth spins us into an alternate reality where the stars have been brought into their proper alignment and Top Jimmy – blues-belter, bar tender and taco vendor – has become a star of TV and radio, if not a sex god who makes the girls scream. After an end-of-the-world guitar solo by Eddie, the song reaches its climax with Roth and Mike Anthony coming across like a couple of swooning teenage girls, as they coo, 'Ohhhhhh, Jimmieeee'.

Partly as a result of their raised profile after the release of Van Halen's song at the turn of 1983–4, Top Jimmy and the Rhythm Pigs were able to release an album, *Pigus Drunkus Maximus* (1987). While Jimmy and Roth had, back in 1984, been thinking of making an album of country tunes, it never came to pass.[25] All he really wanted to do was to make a record that his mother, who ran a roadhouse in Kentucky, would put on her jukebox.

More than fifteen years after the song 'Top Jimmy' was released, Zero-Zero founder John Pochna claimed that Roth mourned the passing of those days so much that he still carried a flimsy and worn Zero-Zero membership card in his wallet.[26] Aside from Van Halen's tribute, the spirit of Top Jimmy (who died in 2001) is captured in the words of Don Waller. 'Truthfully, all I really remember', he said,

> is standing in line outside the Zero-Zero Club, the epicentre of the after-hours Hollywood rock scene . . . Top Jimmy – ometimes X roadie and white blues vocalist extraordinaire – was working the door. This guy comes up and says, 'Hey, man, you gotta let me in. I'm Chris Fradkin. I write songs with the Plimsouls.' Top Jimmy looks down at him through a haze of stubble and blear. 'Yeah? Well, my mama usta fuck the Ink Spots – and she was hip, too – but she ain't gettin' in tonight and you ain't either.'[27]

The Zero-Zero would soon after move to a new location and become the more respectable Zero One (or 0-1) Gallery, this time a proper art space largely dedicated to lowbrow and outsider art (Top Jimmy's ashes, indeed, were put on display there after he died). But to the world beyond Hollywood, Roth's connection to what was happening in Los Angeles in the early 1980s would remain largely unknown. Even in 2003, the *LA Weekly* could mention it within the context of 'little known facts' about the singer when it reported on an opening at the Zero One Gallery:

Lest we forget, forever-young Roth is a product of his environment, Los Angeles. He was a big supporter of the LA punk scene, was an investor in the Zero One art gallery, where many punkers and artists hung out and performed, and was a big-time early booster of the East LA music scene, championing Los Lobos and the Plugz before they started making headway.[28]

Typically, though, Van Halen – as a band – had never been part of this, or any other scene. Their success did, however, inadvertently pave the way for the Los Angeles hard rock and metal scene of the mid-1980s, which featured a number of Van Halen clones, but none with the diverse influences or eccentricity of the original. Roth, however, took an interest in anything going on in Hollywood, and found himself often in the company of Mötley Crüe – introducing them onstage at The Troubadour in 1982. In their best-selling memoir of the decadent life, *The Dirt: Confessions of the World's Most Notorious Rock Band* (2001), he appears as a visitor to what was named the Motley House, situated just down the road from The Whisky A Go Go, partaking of the excess. On one occasion, they recount, he was sitting on the grubby floor so fixated on 'a big pile of blow' that he barely took any notice of a closet door that had come loose and slammed down on his head. 'Dave halted his monologue for half a second and then continued. He didn't seem to be aware that anything out of the ordinary had happened.'[29]

6 THE TAO OF DAVE: SURF LIFE

It is really impossible to appreciate what is meant by the Tao
without becoming, in a rather special sense, stupid.

– Alan Watts, *The Way of Zen*

Writing in 1997, David Lee Roth described the occasion when,
at the age of six, he had decided to go it alone in the world.
After literally falling flat on his face in the schoolyard one day
and having to suffer the taunts of his classmates, he manifested
his sense of isolation from their unkind world in the form of a
model boat, which he had constructed as the means of some
kind of symbolic escape into a better future. It was made from
little bits of wood, with pencils and paper for its sails. 'This is me',
he told himself, as he kicked the little boat off the family porch,
launching it out into the world.[1] As in a shipwreck, it would be
every man for himself from now on.

Soon enough, though, a glimpse of a better future could be
seen during the summers he spent away from school – and away
from other children – in the bohemian quarter of New York's
Greenwich Village in the late 1950s and early '60s. Roth's father
was at the time a medical student completing his training, which
meant a fair amount of moving around the country. The family
had also lived in Indiana and Massachusetts before finally moving
to Southern California in the early 1960s. In Greenwich Village
Roth's guide was his aunt Judy. She was the wife of Manny Roth
– Uncle Manny – the 'tough-talking' owner of the famous Cafe
Wha? night club, once described as an 'enormous dark room at
115 MacDougal Street'.[2] In 1960, the improvised-looking sign at
the side entrance to the basement club bore the legend 'Cafe

Wha? the villages swinginst cafe', with a few more clues to what might be encountered down there splattered underneath in paint:

Beat poets
Jazz crazy bongos
Congos
Live beatniks
Creepnik

In those formative summers, Roth and his father lived in Manny's loft above Bleecker and MacDougal Streets, when the floor of the apartment would often also provide a place for countless musicians and performers – newly arrived in the Village and looking for work – to sleep.[3] Around that time it wasn't unusual to see new singers like Bob Dylan, the comedian (and later, TV star) Bill Cosby, or even Allen Ginsberg and some of the Beat writers and poets – Jack Kerouac, Gregory Corso – at the Cafe Wha?. Some time later, in 1966, Jimi Hendrix would briefly lead the Wha?'s first house band, before being discovered by visiting Animals bassist Chas Chandler, who soon after took the guitarist to London where he would quickly make his legend.

Thus Bob Dylan – in keeping with many of the aspiring performers in those times – was drawn to the Cafe Wha? when he first arrived in Greenwich Village in 1961. The club, as one of Dylan's early influences, Dave Van Ronk, wrote, 'had drags out on the street, pulling customers in . . . it was the best deal for a clyde just off the bus from Kansas City'.[4] Or, as it happened, 'off the bus' from Minnesota, in Dylan's case. 'I worked for Manny all afternoons, from twelve to eight', he wrote in his autobiography of 2001, *Chronicles*: 'I worked the dayshift back then . . . [the Wha?] stayed open from eleven in the morning to four in the [next] morning and there was constantly something happening on the stage.'[5] And it was there, up on the little wooden stage of

Manny Roth's Cafe Wha?, 115 MacDougal Street, Greenwich Village, New York, mid-1960s. The club was where performers such as Bob Dylan, Richie Havens and Jimi Hendrix would start their careers.

the Wha?, that Dylan got a sense of being part of the whole gamut of American entertainment, just another hopeful among a carnivalesque procession of mugging faces, plonking guitars and bad jokes. The club's daytime shows were, as he describes it, a riot of undifferentiated showbiz, as if 100 years of tradition moved like an apparition across the boards. Today we might call this entertainment 'Variety' and, as Dylan notes, to a newcomer it lent the Wha? an air of wondrousness, of being somewhere to which all kinds of misfits could escape, lost in the confusion of their own self-discovery. So, it wasn't unusual, he tells us, to see 'a comedian, a ventriloquist, a steel drum group' – just like that, one after the other. But that wasn't the half of it – there then might be 'a poet, a female impersonator, a duo who sang Broadway stuff', or again,

> a rabbit-in-the-hat magician, a guy wearing a turban who hypnotized people in the audience, somebody whose entire act was facial acrobatics – just anybody who wanted to break into show business.[6]

Being exposed to these surroundings for long periods – all day, every day – it is perhaps no accident that Roth would claim his genealogy among 'show people' – just as, undoubtedly, assorted circus acts, comedians, sideshow wrestlers and, indeed, singers and musicians could. One of the regular performers at the Wha? during this time, who also found himself sleeping on Manny Roth's floor, was Richie Havens, the singer who later – and unforgettably, thanks to the film of the event – opened the Woodstock Festival in 1969. Eight years earlier, in 1961, however, he had arrived in Greenwich Village and ended up, like Dylan and numerous other newcomers, finding his way to the Cafe Wha?, among whose attractions was that it was one of the first places in the Village to start paying folk singers decent money to play.[7] The club 'was no minor-league deal', Havens recalled some years later: 'Not many clubs in New York were doing as much business as the Wha? or were as skilful at milking dollars from their customers. The crowds began pouring in during the afternoon and continued to grow past midnight.'[8] But while there was plenty of work for the performers during the club's extended opening hours, one thing Havens didn't expect, he later remembered, was to be left again and again to entertain Manny Roth's hyperactive nephew, David: 'Manny would come down to the club and say "Hey, Richie, would you look after the kid, I'll be back in half an hour", and then he'd disappear for three hours!'[9] 'And this kid', Havens told a journalist 40-odd years later – barely able to believe it – 'wound up decades later being in this really popular rock band'. And with the sense of incredulity that might be born of half a life of time elapsed, Havens marvelled: 'David Lee Roth. I halfway brought him up!'[10]

Much of the time, however, the young David would be left in the care of Manny's bohemian wife Judy, then barely into her twenties herself, who took him to the kinds of places where he was unlikely to find any other children to play with – quite the contrary, in fact. In bars such as the Cedar Tavern, a well-known watering hole for 1950s artists Willem De Kooning, Robert Motherwell and Jackson Pollock, would be found what most normal parents of those still conservative times might have regarded as a thoroughly bad example for a young boy – artists and writers who would sometimes brawl over petty disputes, or whose turn it was to buy a drink. It made enough of an impression that, for a brief period of time, he decided he would be a painter.[11]

However, by 1963 Roth would leave behind Greenwich Village, as he moved with his parents to California, and was proving so difficult to keep under control that he was taken out of the public school system. After considering the possibility of military school, his parents placed him in the more academic but nonetheless stern and disciplinarian surroundings of the Webb School of California, Claremont. It was an elite prep school whose motto, 'leaders, not ordinary men', set a mood of earnest academic endeavour. There he was faced not with the freewheeling adventures of life in Greenwich Village – the world of Dylan, Kerouac and the bohemian – but the stiff formality of the kind of education preferred by the truly elite. Among his classmates were the offspring of overseas royalty and the sons of eminent industrialists. It was the school where the state governor Ronald Reagan's wayward son, Ron Jr, was sent.

Much in contrast to the kind of school day funhouse he celebrated with Van Halen in the song 'Hot for Teacher' – one in a long history of rock'n'roll songs about school – Roth was confronted with a world that seemed not to belong to the California of The Beach Boys, nor to the world occupied by Hollywood movie stars, but to another time and place altogether. The school was governed by arcane rituals and a social pecking order that meant juniors, such as he was on arrival, deferred in all things to boys a year or so older. Compared to what he had seen in New York, however, they were all nobodies. On top of all that there was the quasi-military seriousness of the English games masters telling him how to do this and that; things he had no interest in. Roth described a rugby coach named 'Ossery M. Butler III, late of the British Navy', who, in the true Corinthian spirit of sporting participation being more important that professional competition, 'smoked a pipe on the field'.[12] It wasn't quite afternoons at the Cafe Wha? with Richie Havens or the beatniks, but it perhaps provided something necessary to rebel against.

Needless to say, the educational experiment had to fail for Roth to find rock'n'roll: he had drunk in too much of the freedom of his bohemian summers in New York with Uncle Manny, and all the rest, and was expelled after little more than a semester for 'failure to adjust' to the Webb school lifestyle.[13]

Roth's failure to 'adjust' arguably extended further; to the way he viewed rock'n'roll, especially within the context of a time when it was either becoming self-consciously serious or bland, formulating itself very neatly to existing formats.

For a decade or so after the initial burst of excitement that fuelled the emergence of rock'n'roll, it was seen largely by outsiders as a brutish, primitive mode of sensory submission that extolled a particular kind of artlessness that just happened to inspire a generation. In this respect, if no other, it was a phenomenon in tune with the Beats – both in terms of its celebrating a childlike immediacy, and the reception it was accorded. Jack Kerouac, the most notable – or infamous – of the Beats, was, after all, dubbed 'an ape with a typewriter' who used 'the strange modern techniques of jive, junk and high speed to achieve his special ecstasy'.[14] John Tytell, in his study of Beat aesthetics, *Naked Angels*, writes:

> When the voice of personality seemed so endangered by an anonymity of sameness, the Beats discovered a natural center for the silence of the day in a new sense of self, a renaissance of the romantic impulse to combat unbelievably superior forces.[15]

Those words, 'the Beats', could easily be replaced by the words 'rock'n'roll'. Just as the Beats, in Tytell's words, 'crashed through the restraining mask of the removed artist', so rock'n'roll initially came to us unadorned by artistic pretensions.[16] Indeed, Kerouac himself wrote, towards the end of his life (he died in 1968), that 'the Beat generation, though dead, was resurrected and justified' in rock'n'roll.[17]

Certainly, what is called rock'n'roll was identified with formal qualities and a more or less typical sound – produced by guitar, bass, drums, piano and saxophone – but the forms rock'n'roll took, based upon such ingredients, became varied enough that eventually it stood for a position in opposition to authority. As W. T. Lhamon notes in his study of cultural aesthetics in the 1950s, *Deliberate Speed* (1990), an 'ideal of Eternal youth' permeated the atmosphere, to the dismay of those who favoured the calm life, and it was all due to rock'n'roll. 'That atmosphere is charged', he notes, 'and wanton squandering of energy – in decibels, pace, and unstable motion – always accompanies it.'[18]

When rock'n'roll grew up and became self-conscious about its art, it was called 'rock' and the elements of play and abandon that had so distinguished it were often lost in seriousness – which is not to say the seriousness itself struck a bum note, or was not often a good thing, but merely that Van Halen – during the Roth years – were always more rock'n'roll than rock; more about play and a kind of spontaneity in attitude than self-conscious stabs at artistry.

Roth's artistic temperament stemmed from somewhere else. Its main characteristic was a childlike artlessness that combined the immediacy of the everyday with the 'no-mind' of Zen. Like Kerouac, for whom 'future ambitions or past memories' were 'an evasion of the immediate', the 'Tao of Dave' involved, as he often said, tearing off the rear view mirror and looking no further than a few metres ahead – 'let's follow the hood ornament'.[19]

Richard Meltzer's *The Aesthetics of Rock* (1987), a sometimes barmy attempt to seek guidance from the likes of Aristotle and Friedrich Nietzsche in confronting the essence of this apparently unrefined, spontaneous and meaningless form of musical expression we call rock'n'roll, settles on examples that seem to express, more than anything else, the immediate – what might also be termed 'the unconscious'. It features, for instance, an extended philosophical digression on the sheer gust of energy that is The Trashmen's 'Surfin' Bird', an obscure garage rock tune from 1963. For anyone who hasn't heard it, this is essentially a couple of minutes of babble, driven by a primal intensity that, precisely, serves to make it timeless. It's a snapshot of a moment; a few minutes in time that, by chance, were captured. For Meltzer such examples illustrated that the fundamentals of rock'n'roll belonged more within the sphere of *passion* than experience; were more about *feeling* than thinking. Rock'n'roll – as such – could not be rationalized, and that was the whole point. It was was, Meltzer thought, possessed of numerous 'unknown tongues', which reached the level of communication perhaps only when the giver and the receiver were primed for that singular connection.

Maybe, therefore, the often-mocked claim of rock'n'roll musicians that performing was difficult to explain, except as something akin to sex, was not so odd. That is because, Meltzer writes:

> An orgasm, as we all know, arises slowly as it builds up and suddenly strikes, leaving one back on earth, but perceptively richer. The compression of neural experience in orgasm is mirrored in rock's compression of eclectically selected elements into juxtapositions which yield unknown tongues.[20]

The 'unknown tongue' might equally be a way to describe the inarticulate, the stupid or dumb. It is the Three Stooges mocking seriousness not by reason, or even necessarily language, but as Kerouac tells us in *On the Road* (1951), through something more basic than that:

> bonk, boing, crash, skittely boom, pow, slam, bang, boom, wham, blam, crack, frap, kerplunk, clatter, clap, blap, fap, slapmap, splat, crunch, crowsh, bong, splat, splat, *BONG!*[21]

In other words, the mere *act* was the thing – and it was more important than what was said or what could be said about it. 'Meaning' was totally irrelevant. As Robert Pattison notes, the aesthetics of rock'n'roll heralded 'the age of vulgarity'.[22] And this partly explains Roth's relationship to the 'peanut gallery' of critics, as we saw in chapter One, which was to mock them, make them work for *his* entertainment. For Roth, rock'n'roll wasn't about the kind of self-expression that, in many ways, spawned the music critic (the one who would chart the arc of an artist's development, in terms of steps towards maturity). Instead, adhering to Zen beliefs in transience, in not striving towards a goal as the means of engaging a creative intelligence that would function best when it was *not* focused, Roth's practice – which, we shouldn't forget –

extended beyond the stage and studio, and accorded to the outline of Zen creativity described by Alan Watts. 'Superior work has the quality of an accident', Watts noted:

> This is not merely a masterful mimicry of the accidental, an assured spontaneity in which the careful planning does not show. It lies at a much deeper and more genuine level, for what the culture of Taoism and Zen proposes is that one might become the kind of person who is a source of marvellous accidents.[23]

Thus, as Roth told *Rolling Stone* in 1979:

> I hate the word *maturing* . . . I don't like the word *evolving*. Or any of that bullshit. The idea is to keep it as simplistic, as innocent, as unassuming and as stupid as possible.[24]

The Zen masters believed, in Watts's reading, that the man of character appears stupid, as if he doesn't know what he is doing, but at the same time is always engaged by such means in bringing into play an 'innate and spontaneous intelligence by using it without forcing it'.[25] Thus the seemingly paradoxical aim was to have no aims, no goals. 'If you want to send a message', Roth would say, 'use Western Union.' As Daisetz Suzuki, propagator of Zen in the USA, wrote in *The Zen Doctrine of No-Mind* (1949):

> The Zen masters all proclaim that there is no enlightenment (satori) whatever which you can claim to have attained. If you say you have attained something, this is the surest proof that you have gone astray.[26]

Roth echoed such sentiments so frequently that a long list of examples could be produced. 'It is the doing I crave', he told one interviewer in 1982: 'People who work towards a goal – the worst thing that can happen is to reach it.'[27] Being true to that spirit involved being aware that the practice of any craft was best realized by avoiding any external goals, which might include success, progress, development or any of the ways we typically try to take the world within our grasp. 'There's a Zen parable about drawing a leaf', Roth told the *Los Angeles Times*:

> Some people draw the leaf with a single line and they just keep making the picture bigger and bigger and bigger. Others will only draw one leaf and over the years they just keep painting smaller and smaller lines inside of it. And that's kind of what Van Halen is doing.[28]

It is an analogy that also, from the point of view of artistic growth as the result of striving for perfection, points to the limitations of Van Halen (when judged by the standards of artistic maturity rather than rock'n'roll exuberance). In the face of success, how long could ambitions stoked by adulation and accolades – that pulled them beyond a simple passion for rock'n'roll as *play* – be resisted?

Nonetheless, the 'Tao of Dave' viewed the music and the *idea* of Van Halen as reflecting the world around them. The aim, in other words, was to catch the moment in true Zen California style; to get caught in the big gust of wind that might take you somewhere interesting and unexpected. What this meant was that the spirit was not channelled through some presumed 'confessional' or self-revealing artistic 'voice' – something that became a lot more common as rock musicians took seriously the opportunities the form offered to be artistic in a way in which a painter or writer might aspire. To be a 'surfer of the moment' was an approach to the practice of craft that was not only in keeping with the Zen doctrine of no-mind – the very 'non-graspingness' of creativity – but is also an orientation to life in more general terms that has been identified, in particular, with a Southern Californian state of mind.

Reyner Banham referred to it as the 'tradition' of Californian 'satori-seeking' – 'satori' being the Buddhist term for 'awakening' or 'enlightenment' – and it was manifested in a diffuse set of practices, attitudes and lifestyles that had in common a way of relating to life and to time – particularly to the future.[29] Here, the future was almost a series of unfolding moments in the present that must not extend too far into the future. It was, in other words, the state of mind characteristic of a culture that was essentially constructed on the idea and ideology of youth and the experience of being young.

Banham was onto something about California that others have also noted: the propensity to let go – of the past, of traditions, and of inhibitions. When Roth took off in flight onstage there was something going on there that was not as simple as a guy just jumping up and down to rock'n'roll music (say, in the way that Pete Townshend of The Who did, pounding the floor as he leapt with his knees bent up to his chest, and down – BAM – as a kind of punctuation that was quite violent in its intent). With Townshend, this was his music, and he owned it, he was stomping on it to show his mastery over it. But there was, in all seriousness, something Zen about Roth's flights into the air. He seemed to be sailing through invisible currents, and in-between or on top of whatever the music was doing – he wasn't moving to the music, in other words but, rather, taking off from it. Was he not, in fact, riding it? 'Hanging Ten' like a surfer, but on the sonic waves, that he sang of in 'On Fire' back in 1978?

As already mentioned, 'Hanging Ten' is one of the most revered, and difficult, surf moves – balancing on the very tip of the surfboard – which makes it look as though the surfer has almost become at one with the wave. And it might easily be related to the Zen aesthetics of spontaneity, of enlightenment found in the moment, that Reyner Banham had thought was so Californian, so evident in surfing and hang-gliding, for instance. Those activities (not 'sports', per se) exemplify 'non-graspingness' and make surfing a suitable art for the practice of Zen. Consider this, an observation by Sanford Kwinter, who was trying to understand the singularity of what, philosophically, is termed 'the event':

> Surfers do not conceive of themselves as exclusive or 'prime movers' at the origin of their movements, they rather track, from within the flows, a variety of emerging features, singularities, and unfoldings with which they can meld.[30]

Roth, in that very sense, sought to get caught in 'events'. He might coast through the air like some beach-bum-cum-samurai-warrior, but what is curious is that it was in a manner that had nothing as a precedent in rock'n'roll; which is just to say, it belonged somewhere else entirely. In later years, after leaving Van Halen, he began doing something else that was very interesting. He would twirl a katana (a ceremonial Samurai sword) – glinting in the light – it was silver, like the shaft of a microphone stand – around his static body with such speed and dexterity that to the naked eye it seemed to take on a form and shape defined by the contours of the movement – a blur of steely motion as he remained more-or-less still at the centre. This was derived from fifteenth-century Samurai moves that Roth had learned during the martial arts training he had been undertaking since he was twelve years old. Images of this – especially moving images – suggest the kind of effect that Futurist sculpture of the early twentieth century was after: where a body could appear simultaneously frozen and in motion.

When Roth directed his Zen leanings towards his songwriting he was pushed closer into the area occupied by those who created meaningless and trashy rock'n'roll – Zen rock'n'roll – where he found more common ground with the flash-in-the-pan effervescence of teen pop than the avowedly 'serious' songwriters who might view music as a means of self-exploration. Pop music was transient – it embodied, for good or bad, what was true of a time and place. And, as someone who once claimed that he could dream only about attaining the transient status of 'trash', Roth was – unsurprisingly – well aware of the implications of such an 'aesthetics' of the moment. The truth was that anything that was in tune with the moment necessarily touched a reality that would always be subject to change, particularly – as in Roth's case – under the weight of forces one didn't seek to control. 'I believe in disposable culture, because it's significant of the time and place it occurs in', he told Mick Brown of the *Sunday Times Magazine* in 1984:

> Van Halen – any rock band – is a historical paragraph. It's disposable not because it's bad – although these things often are – but because there are so many new things coming along and replacing it. I support that.[31]

For many, this was a kind of self-effacement that would make Roth's own work something less than artistic; these were sentiments, after all, that seemed to deny an idea of cultural durability that is usually held to be the hallmark of all great art.

What Roth exemplified, however, was ambiguity, which was one quality that seemed to lie beyond the grasp of some critics. His comfort with ambiguity, with self-negation – and as Alan Watts notes, Zen takes 'positive delight' in the void – represented not only the denial of that 1970s idea of rock's cultural significance, but its emerging institutional structure, which in turn presumed to add credence to its cultural significance.[32] Roth thought this a 'morbid country club' that sought to impose a 'code of ethics'.[33] His Zen rock'n'roll was – like the 'unknown tongues' Richard Meltzer celebrated – 'stupid' in the Zen sense of being inscrutable:

not open to the kind of examination that was destroying the aura
of music as event, which is to say the critical pursuit of 'meaning':
'You can't break [a song] down into exactly . . . *what does it mean?*',
he told Steven Rosen in 1980. 'Cos I wrote the fuckin' thing and
I don't even know! But it *feels* good. If it *feels* good, then it just *is*.'[34]
And to the critic-interviewer, Roth pointedly expressed the futility
of looking for such answers by chuckling his way through an
impromptu chorus of Bob Dylan's 'Ballad of a Thin Man':

> There's something happening
> And *you* don't know what it is
> Do *you*, Mr Jones

'And that', he added, 'was the whole point of Van Halen'; to strive
to keep from developing a self-consciousness that might negate
the band's openness to feeling – to the very world it inhabited.

The 'Tao of Dave' animates a series of albums made between
1977 and 1983. They were approached in a spirit of looseness –
1970s looseness – that etched the 'mistakes' that other bands
would remove *into* the grooves of their records. 'All the best
parts of our music are just made up on the spot', Roth said.[35] '
You can't take things *too* seriously or you become *elite*. You start
to become special or different or – even worse – *better*.'[36] At such
times Van Halen became something like pop art as performance,
a confusion of cultural sources that would come to life as an event:

> A lot of the things you see up onstage really have nothing
> to do with archetypal rock and roll . . . It's vaudeville. It's
> ballet. It's ESPN full-contact karate. It's tap dancing. It's Henry
> Youngman. It's everything. You pile it all up together and make
> a great big stew out of it.[37]

That was the source of improvisation – not musical improvisation, as such, but improvisation in the sense of making it up as the situation played itself out. Why else would Roth be drawn to, and be so at home in, the lexicon of jive? But, as Tytell notes in *Naked Angels*, the jive-talker 'would improvise his facts, confuse his cultural sources . . . [as] part of a necessary disguise'.[38] Such a disguise concealed the artistic 'I', or the meanin

g that critics were so keen to uncover. When interviewers asked how he would describe Van Halen, Roth would say – 'as a mixture of ice hockey and religion'. But, for all that – for all 'his fast-yap, quick-from-

the-lip jive' – as Peter Goddard wrote in 1984, 'Roth may be more of an artist than he or any of his zillion critics will ever let on'. The combination of Zen Roth with the often 'out-there' musicality of Eddie Van Halen made them, Goddard thought, perhaps 'the most radical band now playing in America'.[39]

Goddard leapt on what he termed one of Roth's 'Zen-burger' philosophical nuggets as being a lot more important than the way the singer threw it out might have suggested – 'I am merely the pond that reflects the oncoming stone'. That was his response to the question of how Van Halen's live performances unfolded. Goddard was the jazz and pop critic of the *Toronto Star* and what he saw onstage seemed quite 'out there'. 'This kind of stuff is frightfully hard to come to grips with', he said:

> For one thing, it doesn't *want* to be analyzed; for another, it often happens so loudly, so quickly, it'd be just as easy to analyze a gust of air. Something of a similar problem is faced by critics of avant-garde classical music. Sure you can break the thing down into its various parts, but that's only long after the event itself is over. And the event is the thing![40]

To be in the midst of that – this 'gust of air', this 'event', as

Goddard said – was, for Roth, the whole deal. It was arguably why Roth-era Van Halen never made a live record, because you had *to be there*, or you missed something of the essence of it; the things that microphones didn't capture – that 'great big stew' spread out over the stage.[41]

As the Zen master Daisetz Suzuki said in his consideration of archery, the archer needs to lose the self-consciousness that would separate him from his bow and arrow in order to become at one with it. In Zen-like rock'n'roll the point was to enter a different kind of temporality, losing oneself in some larger consciousness that would release the performer from whatever it was that kept them and the audience separate. 'When people scream so hysterically for such a sustained period of time', Roth told *Rolling Stone* in 1984, 'they're screaming for themselves. Not for me. Not because Eddie is so great. But because they see themselves reflected in us.'[42]

Being of 'no-mind', in the Zen way, was therefore of utmost importance. Being 'stupid', being about 'nothing' and not believing in the notion of art as self-consciously revealing an interior 'self' made the vital connection with the audience for the duration of those 'events' and beyond. There was a danger in forgetting this, Roth thought, because the laws of magic depend on withholding a certain amount of the art:

> Look, it's like that old magic axiom – all the people are going to ask you about the mirrors and the wires. They want to know so badly [but] the second you tell 'em, they think, what a sap.[43]

Being stupid, in the sense understood by Zen was, as Alan Watts says, 'not to reduce the human mind to a moronic vacuity' but to ensure creativity could remain in tune with the mind's 'peripheral vision', able to 'feel' out a situation.[44]

This was all illustrated in an interview aired on American TV's *Entertainment Tonight* show in 1981, and conducted with Roth significantly seen languishing in bed at his apartment just off the Sunset Strip. The straight-laced and sincere presenter, clearly assuming that Van Halen's success and their music must have some driving aim behind it, asked him a question along the lines of 'what are your songs about?'. It was the wrong question to ask, in a way, but as he lay there in his ripped T-shirt and aviator shades, Roth began to work up one of his characteristic jive diversions – which rambled through the relative merits of chilli dogs, Rastafarianism, punk rock and Rolls-Royce cars – without addressing the question. He picked up a guitar that was on the bed next to him and plucked three notes as he deadpanned to the camera: 'this is how a *banker* plays the guitar.' As the twang of the last note was still ringing out, he suddenly launches the guitar off into the air and out of view of the TV camera. As it crash-lands in the near distance with a dull *ttthhhhudd,* he says, right on cue: 'And that is how a rock'n'roller plays guitar.'

It was squarely in keeping with the attitude of someone like Kerouac who, as Gerald Nicosia recalls, would babble and sing nonsense songs when television interviewers tried to get him to say what it all *meant*, this Beat thing. On one occasion, indeed, Kerouac 'gave Zen answers' to a barrage of intellectual questions posed by students at a public appearance, Nicosia says, and resorted to making 'sounds like a child by slapping his finger against his lips'.[45] That, in many ways, was Roth's aesthetic, too.

opposite: 'This is a soundtrack for something, and I dunno what. There's a lot I don't know about this stuff. That's the beauty of it . . . I propose the toasts.' David Lee Roth onstage, Miami, Florida, December 1982.

7 DIVER DOWN, TEMPERATURE UP, *c.* 1981–2

Yasutani reminds us that there is no fixed 'I'. The pure or original self 'is like the ocean, and each individual is a wave on the surface of the ocean'.

– Thomas Farber, *The Face of the Deep*

If Zen can be characterized, among a variety of qualities, as Alan Watts wrote, by 'directness, verve and humor and a sense of both beauty and nonsense at once exasperating and delightful' then *Diver Down*, more than any of Van Halen's albums, may be their – or David Lee Roth's – flawed Zen gift to posterity.[1] When it was released in 1982 Warner Bros ran an advert with the words 'Diver Down, Temperature Up' above a photo of a busty waitress delivering the new 'platter' on – well – a platter. If only it had been that obvious.

The cover of the album and the title, as Roth said at the time, had naval connotations – the red background with the white diagonal slash that was on the front of the album was actually the signal flag that was hoisted on a boat when a diver had gone overboard. For Roth, and for this album, it meant that there was something going on that wasn't apparent on the surface. No kidding. In retrospect, it seems clear that *Diver Down* became the first serious gambit in a contest between Eddie Van Halen and Roth for supremacy over the direction of the band, one that would end with Roth walking out on Van Halen in April 1985. When seen in this light, *Diver Down* documented not only their varied influences but also their musical differences. It was a mish-mash, but one quite in keeping with the idea that to be Californian was to be, in a sense, an admixture of apparently incompatible elements and traits. Reyner Banham, for instance, once observed that Los

Angeles itself seemed to have been created as the result of some
kind of mischief; as if North America had been tipped on its side
until everything that wasn't fixed down found itself scattered
across the great city.[2] That same kind of playfulness might have
produced *Diver Down*, an album that recalls Roth's description
of Van Halen's live show in 1980; 'it's a hodgepodge – we'll just
throw some stuff in and see where it lands' – and indeed his
description of the 'big stew' of influences that made it all work.
'Too confusing for anybody but Van Halen', wrote Dave Queen,
in an amusing reassessment of the album some years later:

> *Diver Down* (where pothead singer David Lee Roth took over)
> included five cover versions – with its additional fragments,
> sketches, and impenetrable arcana, *Diver Down* is like an 'un-
> official' Fall release or *Smiley Smile*. To appease the guitarist, a
> detail of his famous adhesive taped guitar was the cover art.[3]

That last detail was a joke, of course. While *Diver Down* wasn't
quite as unconsidered as any random album by The Fall, it was
perhaps more like The Beach Boys' infamous *Smiley Smile*, which
Timothy White wrote was 'taken by many true believers to be a
veritable slap in the face' – as if The Beach Boys 'had made an
album for tots'.[4] In a way, this also describes *Diver Down*, where
Roth's childlike unconscious seemed to rule.

'Van Halen's an unusual hybrid', Roth once said. 'If it was a plant,
I could see why some people might not go near it.'[5] Musically, the
result of this entity was sometimes betwixt and between what
most observers would regard as two – or more – unbridgeable
points. 'It's not heavy metal and it's not The Temptations,' Roth
told one interviewer, 'but it's something in between.'[6] However by
the time of *Diver Down* even that formulation was too reductive,
perhaps even a bit misleading.

An insight into Roth's eclecticism was glimpsed in an interview from 1984, when a journalist from *Record* magazine, curious to know what music the singer was then listening to, made a note of the assortment of cassettes lying around his hotel room – she found some Clifton Chenier (the Zydeco accordionist), Black Uhuru (the dub reggae group), Mississippi John Hurt (the country blues-folk singer), as well as a tape of *An Evening with Groucho Marx*.[7] Roth claimed that the way he sang couldn't be disentangled from his influences, from the music he had always listened to, which was 'Motown, disco and Jelly Roll blues: Big Joe Turner, Howlin' Wolf, Muddy Waters'.[8] His were a set of tastes not always shared by Eddie Van Halen – Roth 'loved disco', Eddie once said in an interview in 1996, as if to demonstrate the singer's lack of serious-ness: 'probably still does'.[9] Yet as Eddie also admitted, it was the contrast between the two men, and their divergent influences, that largely accounted for the band's success.[10]

Writing in *Creem* magazine in 1980, Dave DiMartino caught a sense of their not really fitting in when he wondered why it was he could be so fond of Van Halen when he actively hated almost every other rock act – Judas Priest, The Scorpions, Ted Nugent, Rush and so on – that they were typically lumped together with at the time. The answer, he thought, was in the songs. 'Songs are what it boils down to, and Van Halen write great POP songs', he wrote.[11] And, at the heart of those songs, as seems to be the case with so many bands, there were essentially two writers – Eddie Van Halen and David Lee Roth – although the process of crafting those songs into recordings appears to have involved all band members contributing in an editorial sense; making suggestions about arrangements and so on.

The two maybe even disliked each other for a long time in the band's early days, but in terms of musical interests and influences, it seemed more clear-cut – they were like chalk and cheese. It is interesting to recall the tale of how Mick Jagger and Keith Richards

David Lee Roth (left)
and Eddie Van Halen,
post-show, 1982.

Bottoms up!

WELL, IS **David Lee Roth** *of* **Van Halen** *proving at last that*
'there's gold in them there hills' — or merely modelling the latest
recession-inspired 'economy style' leather strides? Certainly **Eddie**
Van Halen *(right) appears equally willing to bare all.*
*   The cheek of the man! Or should we say cheeks. . .?*

– long-lost childhood pals – met some years later only to bond
again over the Chicago blues and rock'n'roll they both loved,
which led to the formation of The Rolling Stones. It might be
the case, in fact, that most rock bands begin at least with shared
musical likes. Not so with Roth and Van Halen. A revealing episode
from the time the two spent as students at Pasadena City College
– between 1972 and 1974 – underlines their differences and hints
at what they respectively brought, in terms of influences and
temperament, to what would become Van Halen.

For a class exam on vocal technique, they were both tasked
with selecting and then performing a song of their choice in front
of the other students. Eddie chose 'Can't Find My Way Home' by
Blind Faith, one of Eric Clapton's short-lived bands; a song that
expressed a serious sentiment in the soul-bearing mode of late
1960s/early 1970s rock. As Roth recalled later, Eddie – who had
actually taken up the role of lead singer before hooking up with
Roth – sang and played guitar 'exactly like it was on the record'.[12]
For his part, Roth sought to impress in an altogether different
way with a rendition of Donny Osmond's hit version of 'Go
Away, Little Girl' from 1971. *Donny Osmond?!* This wasn't even
remotely within the vicinity of cool. Nor was it rock'n'roll but,
rather, the cry of a pleading pubescent seemingly designed to do
little more than make teenage girls scream and faint. Thus it was
that the apparently disparate elements that would come to make
(and arguably break) Van Halen first revealed themselves in public.

Listen now to 'Jamie's Cryin', a song on Van Halen's debut
album of 1978 – and, in particular, to the vocal arrangement –
and try to convince yourself that this is *not* a song that might have
been perfect for some identikit, suit-wearing, vocal harmony pop
group whose target audience was teenage girls. In other words –
The Osmonds! The pop influence in Van Halen's music, however,
is where they depart from, say, the Californian hard-rock template
of *Montrose* (1973), the album produced by Ted Templeman for the

band of the same name, which Van Halen bear only a superficial resemblance to the closer one looks. The melodic pop element and, particularly, the vocal arrangements and performances belong somewhere else. In addition to that, the hard rock element, especially on *Van Halen* (1978) seemed to soar on the jet stream; it suggested – contrary to its simplicity – something that was state of the art. *Rolling Stone* magazine equivocated about the merits of Van Halen, but nonetheless sensed that they belonged to a new, faster and more energetic breed of hard rock and possessed 'the hormones' to supersede predecessors who had 'become fat and self-indulgent and disgusting.'[13]

That's all to say that Van Halen's combination of pop and hard rock, together with a certain unreserved expenditure of energy, was what set them apart from the world of hard rock and heavy metal they became associated with. The difference was that they had the wit, for a time, and the confidence – the lack of self-consciousness – just to throw anything into the mix that seemed to fit, no matter whether or not the elements were supposed to go together. And despite the emphasis given to Eddie's guitar work, it is just as much in the vocal arrangements as in the instrumental parts that simplistic genre expectations were swept aside.

On 'I'm the One' (1978), for example, there is a vocal breakdown that it would be hard to imagine any other bunch of long-haired leather-wearing rockers attempting and which sets Van Halen apart from their most immediate hard rock predecessors. It builds gradually from Roth's lone voice, which intones a familiar-sounding 1950s-style vocal lick:

ba ba da
shooby doo wah
ba ba da
shooby doo wah

It then includes two, three and more voices adding bass and a counterpoint line, *ba da da*, performed by the rest of the band (and perhaps Ted Templeman), which builds and overlaps within the space of seventeen seconds to sound like a full-on barbershop ensemble – or perhaps something that might have been found within the grooves of a record by Templeman's old band, Harpers Bizarre. It also seemed like another example of a kind of natural exuberance that located this band in a distinctive place and culture – California. As Carey McWilliams wrote, California presents 'a reality that at first seems weirdly out of scale, off balance, and full of fanciful distortion'.[14] In a similar way, 'I'm the One' is amazing and monstrous in proportion at the same time – it sounds about ready to explode under the pressure of its inflated, hyperkinetic drive.

Other weird songs include 'Beautiful Girls' (*Van Halen II*, 1979), which features yet another unusual vocal arrangement and performance that seems barely connected to rock'n'roll. A Broadway show tune seems a more apt kind of comparison – vocally it is more like a performance that could have accompanied a latter-day remake of a Busby Berkeley musical or, indeed, the kind of sub-Broadway pop that Rufus Wainwright would come up with.

More generally, however, Van Halen depart from hard-rock norms in that they never became mystical; they never lapsed into ballad territory either. Whereas half of Led Zeppelin's recorded output seems to have been folk-influenced, and often resulted lyrically in such Tolkienesque epics as 'The Battle of Evermore', or folk-tinged hippy tunes like 'Going to California', Van Halen never really had the inclination. Instead they would pull out something like 'Could This Be Magic?' (1980), a song that dropped the electric guitars and speed in favour of something light and acoustic: a sea shanty. What rock bands wrote sea shanties? That song, which spoke of being out on the ocean on a summer's night was, in a way, an accurate summation of where Van Halen always figured in relation to what was going on around them musically – always cut adrift from genre-bound bands who had a firm grasp on where they were headed. With Van Halen, it seems that the opposite was true – they just *went*. As was the case on Sunset Strip in the 1970s, they occupied their own little floating 'island', even if – at times – it was a leaky boat with no oars.

The truth was, though, that Roth – if anyone – seemed willing to grab the oars and take Van Halen somewhere, anywhere, even if it was into the baffling waters of *Diver Down* where only he, perhaps, could see what was going on below the surface. As David Fricke wrote in a profile of a post-Roth Van Halen in 1986, the surprising truth – given Eddie's leading musical role – was that, in addition to providing the main public face of Van Halen, Roth ended up playing 'generalissimo in music matters'.[15] While the band had always seemed to manifest a genuine camaraderie that came across in both the live shows and on record, by 1983 the reality was becoming more complicated, as Eddie sought to regain control of the band from Roth and Templeman's influence.

Before the making of *Fair Warning* (1981), Roth had moved to an apartment block just off the Sunset Strip on Shoreham Drive (a few minutes walk from The Whisky A Go Go in one direction and Sunset Sound Recorders in the other). His Hollywood nightlife presents an interesting contrast with the increasing domesticity of Eddie Van Halen's life (he had married in early 1981), which arguably altered the dynamics of the band. 'People don't just get married and picked out of a herd like cattle', Roth said years later. 'You are aiming in a new direction. You're on a different on-ramp.'[16] This was true, but the real differences were in how the band should approach the recording process – it was the age-old rock'n'roll issue of 'musical differences' that would emerge from the creation of *Diver Down*.

In musical terms, Eddie felt that the *Fair Warning* album's relative lack of success was being put down to the fact that he had assumed too much control over its making. It was a platinum album, but had been a slower seller than previous albums and contained no Top 40 hits, something Warner Bros were increasingly interested in. This led, in Eddie's view, to Roth and Templeman taking even more of a controlling hand for the following year's *Diver Down* album, which sold something in the region of two to three times more copies than *Fair Warning*, and mainly off the back of some hits. The album's reliance on cover versions (of songs by The Kinks, Roy Orbison and Martha Reeves and the Vandellas) sat uneasily with Eddie's growing creative ambitions and his sense that he was losing control of the band he had formed, and of which he was the chief musical brains.

While Eddie was initially supportive of *Diver Down* in public, he would eventually – and repeatedly, as the years passed – slight it, seeming almost to disown it. This was despite the fact that Roth had found an old song, 'Big Bad Bill (is Sweet William Now)' that – true to his eclectic tastes – had previously been recorded by the likes of Judy Garland and Peggy Lee, and which allowed Alex and Eddie Van Halen to make their one and only known recording with their father, who played the clarinet part on the song.

However, beyond the fact that Eddie's lack of interest in the album allowed Roth to assume more control, it was the circumstances of the album's making – from a production point of view – that just seemed to gnaw away at the guitarist in the months to come. He bemoaned the fact that Templeman and Roth bounced him into the studio first to cut a single, which then ended up quickly becoming an entire album, *Diver Down*, half-filled with cover tunes. In truth, the 'no cover songs' plea was an overreaction because some of these songs, like 'Big Bad Bill' and the cover of the Roy Rogers cowboy farewell, 'Happy Trails', were more like interludes or cameos, in an album that seemed more akin to a 'rarities and B-sides' kind of affair. If thought about in those terms, it is a marvellous testament to their unique blend of influences – it just so happens that it presents these influences rather less blended together than ever before in their work. So, what we find is Roth doing his best Louis Armstrong impression on 'Big Bad Bill', Eddie making a guitar sound like a church organ on 'Cathedral' or doing a passable imitation of flamenco guitarist Carlos Montoya on 'Little Guitars (Intro)'. It was all, truly, in the spirit of what separated Van Halen from other bands.

But the one song that stuck in Eddie's craw the most was their cover of Martha Reeves and the Vandellas' 'Dancing in the Street'. What was most interesting about it was that it – in fact – had been turned into a Van Halen tune. Its only real resemblance to the original is in the vocal melody, which remains faithful, if carried at a slightly slower tempo. Underneath Roth's vocal is a pulsating Minimoog riff that Eddie seems to be *squeezing* through an echo-box and a pitch-shifter, with a squealing guitar cut-in for complimentary effect. It is as if someone had plugged Donna Summer's 'I Feel Love' into Eddie's ears as he slept, and this was what he remembered on waking. The beat and rhythm (on bass and drums) are more syncopated, less machinic and softer than the brutal industrial pulse of 'I Feel Love' – yet, more than anything else, nothing like the original version of 'Dancing in the Street'.

But Eddie's one legitimate gripe would have been that he got no credit – certainly not in the publishing – for his contribution whatsoever. From the guitarist's point of view, however, the main problem with this song was that Templeman and Roth had 'stolen' his original piece of music to use on it: 'I fucking hated that song. I never wanted to do it . . . Ted and Roth thought I was out of control on *Fair Warning* . . . and the label wanted a hit single, and they dug up all these cover tunes to try and get a hit.'[17]

Roth, predictably enough, took a different view. For him what was important and would be remembered most of all was the *spirit* of what Van Halen did – and whether or not the music could capture that – not the specifics of who wrote the songs. This was partly because, as he said to Steven Rosen, 'even the songs that were by other people sounded like Van Halen'.[18] 'It's the same thing as stealing hubcaps', he said, dismissively: sure, its true that they may have *belonged* to someone else to begin with, but 'pretty soon they're on your car' – where they look like they always belonged.[19]

Eddie wasn't just on a collision course with Roth, however, but also with Templeman and Warner Bros records. Like other artist-centred labels whose A&R strategy was established in the freewheeling days of the late 1960s and early '70s – other notables included David Geffen's Asylum – Warner Bros enjoyed a reputation as a hip label with a family atmosphere, which fostered a belief that record sales should not, in every case, be the sole criterion of an artist's worth. However, this was a philosophy that was applied unevenly. Warners' artists like Ry Cooder, Van Dyke Parks and Randy Newman, for instance, enjoyed a special status within the company – and were lucky if their album sales nudged into the high tens of thousands – but most of the artists on the label signed after the mid-1970s, and the industry-wide slump in sales, did not.

When Van Halen signed with the label in 1977 the record industry was already entering a period of relative decline. This meant that the company's biggest-selling acts – including Van Halen – would inevitably help to bankroll the company's A&R strategy, which preserved in some cases the kind of art-before-commerce ethos that applied to its so-called 'prestige' artists.[20] Those artists were free to do what they wanted, regardless of commercial pressures. By 1983, however, Eddie thought that Van Halen's success had earned him the right to a greater degree of control over his music. As Alex Van Halen later told *Blender* magazine, Eddie responded by building his own studio because he wanted a clubhouse where he could experiment at any time and [where] there wasn't a clock running. The record company wasn't thrilled about the idea, because they always think that bands are a bunch of drug addicts who need a babysitter. But we had the clout to do it.[21]

It would be the beginning of the end of the Templeman-Roth 'fast'n'dirty' approach, which also heralded a move from the commercial studios of the Sunset Boulevard-Hollywood area to Eddie's house in the Los Angeles canyons.

When it came to the design of this new studio, however, Eddie maintained a connection with Hollywood's famed hit factories. With the help of Donn Landee, who became an integral part of the crafting of the *MCMLXXXIV/1984* album (released in late 1983), he would be much freer than he had ever been to follow his musical instincts and put the thoughts of what the rest of the band wanted out of his mind, even if it meant laying down the tracks himself before presenting them to Ted Templeman and the others. During the recording and mixing of the album, between May and October of 1983, Eddie and Landee knew that it was the studio they had built high in the Hollywood Hills – as much as the music that would be made in it – that would ultimately be on trial. It had to pass muster in order to justify new working arrangements that, to some extent, would sideline Roth and Ted Templeman.

Landee, along with Eddie, designed the studio to try to repli-cate the sound of some of his favoured Los Angeles studios. He rescued a discarded recording console that had previously been used in the United Western studios on Sunset Boulevard. The sixteen-track recorder, designed by Bill Putnam (a pioneer of studio recording in the 1950s who also designed and built the original console at Sunset Sound) was revived by Landee to get the required analogue tube vibe for the new studio at a time when digital recording was supposed to be the new state of the art (fellow Warner Bros artist Ry Cooder had released the first all-digital album in 1979, titled *Bop Till You Drop*). It is more than likely that Templeman and Landee had actually recorded and mixed sessions on the very same piece of equipment before United Western junked it in favour of newer technology. While it was still in use there it had an impeccable Los Angeles pedigree, and was probably used on sessions by The Beach Boys, Phil Spector and The Mamas and the Papas, among the many others who recorded at United Western in the mid- to late 1960s.

But when Eddie bought this as the centrepiece of his new studio for a mere $6,000 it was considered an obsolete relic of a bygone age. It had the military green look of those filing cabinets from the 1960s that used to be seen in offices the world over. To all intents and purposes it looked, he said, like a 'piece of shit . . . with big old knobs and tubes'.[22] By the late 1970s multi-track recording had advanced beyond this kind of sixteen-track equipment, which was state of the art, 1968-style. As it happened, the new studio was decidedly primitive when compared to some of the other musician-owned studios nestling in the Hollywood Hills. One of these was Frank Zappa's new Laurel Canyon facility, where Eddie had found himself the previous spring. It was there that he had hatched the idea to build his own studio and make it the location for the recording of the band's next album.

8 THINK LIKE THE WAVES, LIKE A CHILD, *c.* 1982–3

> The only people for me are the mad ones . . . the ones
> who never yawn or say a commonplace thing, but burn,
> burn, burn.
>
> – Jack Kerouac, *On the Road*

One spring day in 1982, shortly after the release of Van Halen's
Diver Down album, Eddie Van Halen hopped in his Jeep and took
the short ride along Mulholland Drive from his new home on
Coldwater Canyon Avenue to Frank Zappa's studio in Laurel
Canyon. It would be a chance to meet the man who had recently
thanked him for 'reinventing' the guitar. As it turned out, it would
be a more auspicious meeting than he might have ever imagined.
What he saw in the basement of the Zappa family house seemed
to be the solution to many of his problems, as it became clear how
Zappa had always seemed to operate under conditions of total
freedom and was able to record music any time he felt like it –
without either the constraints imposed by other people or the
worry of running up huge bills in commercial studios. At this,
their first meeting, Eddie jammed with Zappa, his then guitarist
Steve Vai and Zappa's twelve-year-old son, Dweezil, who – it turned
out – had been trying to learn some choice Van Halen licks.

Van Halen weren't due to go out on tour until July, so Eddie
ended up spending the best part of a month – during May and
June 1982 – going over to the so-called 'Utility Muffin Research
Kitchen' (as the studio was known) with Van Halen's engineer
Donn Landee to produce a single titled 'My Mother is a Space
Cadet' for Dweezil and his band.

During the sessions Eddie and Landee were occasionally
dumbfounded by the challenge of making a record with a

bunch of twelve-year-olds who really had no idea what they were doing. The two sat behind the console watching the uncontrollable energy of five tearaways who were barely able to keep time, let alone play their instruments. Dweezil later remembered that Eddie would come out and stand in front of them at the beginning of a take, gesturing with his hands as he shouted: 'All right, now . . . GO!' It was as if he was starting off a go-cart race, but it was the only way he could think of to get them to begin playing at the same time.[1] In the end Eddie and Landee had their work cut out to make something from the chaotic fumblings they had captured on tape, but they still had great fun doing it. What was more important was the sense of the studio as a place for trying things out and experimenting – it was an idea that was beginning to take hold of Eddie who, during the making of the previous two Van Halen albums, grew tired of being rushed in and out of the studio in a matter of days or weeks.

During those days driving over the canyons to Zappa's house, the idea to build a new studio at his home took hold. The aim was to build it in time for the recording of the band's next album, which they were due to begin work on in early 1983.

The recording of Van Halen's *MCMLXXXIV/1984* album at Eddie's new studio was interrupted by preparations for a giant outdoor show, the Us Festival at Devore, California (the festival was named '*us*' as in 'we', not US, as in United States). A few weeks before the event, and to celebrate the fact that it coincided with Memorial Day, they enlisted Neil Zlozower, who had worked with the band regularly since 1978, to take some shots that would see them – these non-history men who lived in the moment – identify themselves with history. As they stumbled over dirty hillsides in the Los Angeles canyons, and up by the side of tight and winding roads, passing motorists would have spotted a dishevelled troop of what looked like US marines – except for the overlong hair and a distinct lack of co-ordination.

The plan was to recreate the iconic image of marines raising a flag on Mount Suribachi during the Battle of Iwo Jima in 1945. Zlozower's photograph – a near faithful recreation of the original – appeared as a poster bearing the words 'Van Halen Memorial Day '83', which seemed to distance the band from both the Us Festival and the 'studs'n'leather' acts they were sharing the stage with – they would headline 'Heavy Metal Day', one of four themed days at the festival. Neither Roth nor Eddie appreciated being lumped in with the then exploding heavy metal scene, and claimed not to even know who the other bands on the bill were until they reached the venue. 'Eddie Van Halen Drops the Bomb on Heavy Metal', one magazine reported after the event. Roth, who – just like Eddie – had by this time spawned a host of imitators, had always sought to distance himself from a generation of bands he dubbed 'bastard sons'. Heavy Metal, he thought,

> conjures up polyvinyl chloride times studs times Judas Priest times bondage times a lot of red lights, and on and on. I don't think Van Halen is any of that . . . our sense of humor is too expansive to deal with that seriousness. In every picture of every Heavy Metal guy, he's snarling at you and making his hand into a claw, like he's gonna just *tear your wallet right off your body!*[2]

He held a particular disdain for the opening band on that Heavy Metal Day, Quiet Riot; a Los Angeles outfit who had arrived on the Sunset Strip a year or two after Van Halen in the mid-1970s and whose singer was always keen to suggest that his band – rather than Van Halen – were kings of the Hollywood scene. The fact that Quiet Riot were at the top of the album charts that summer of 1983, only intensified the insults. 'What's the great shakes when your first three albums die a horrifying death and all of a sudden you come in with a big winner?' Roth said: 'Particularly when it's based on somebody else's song that was a semi-hit ten years ago . . . I can speak very authoritatively about this because we did it!'[3]

As Van Halen rolled across the US on tour during 1984, Roth would routinely have a dig at Quiet Riot from the stage every single night, as he took a drink between songs. 'I wanna say that this is real whisky here. This ain't Quiet fuckin' Riot.'

Zlozower's Memorial Day image also lived up to Roth's idea of the band as a roving band of brothers who got into rock'n'roll so they could, as he once said, 'yuk it up like a buncha gypsies in the Foreign Legion'.[4] It shows Alex Van Halen, Eddie and Michael Anthony behind a gun-toting Roth who peers out yonder to the wasteland, like an ever-vigilant Audie Murphy, ready to take on all challengers who would seek to knock Van Halen off their now lofty perch at the top the rock'n'roll heap – their fee for the show would see them ranked in the *Guinness Book of Records* at the end of the year as the highest-paid band in history, having earned $1.5 million for a two-hour show.

Quiet Riot, however, were a minor irritant compared to one of the other headlining acts at the Us Festival, The Clash, who started a feud with Van Halen that served only to illustrate their divergent rock'n'roll aesthetics. Before the event even got under way, Joe Strummer, singer with The Clash, began to get itchy feet about appearing at an event that was probably threatening to upset his band's street cred. Where Roth looked forward to the event as an excuse for a grand celebration, and bemoaned the fact that he wasn't sharing the bill with Culture Club, Strummer and others associated with The Clash attended the carefully orchestrated press events seemingly in denial of the situation. In truth, the whole Us Festival seemed not only distant from Strummer's punk principles but also the neo-hippie 'us generation' talk of the organizers, which looked more and more like empty rhetoric as the festival approached. 'You are going to be part of an event so big, so different it will begin a whole new chapter in the history of live music', the Us promo materials ran: 'We will be joining together in a celebration that will mark the end of the "me" decade and the beginning of the "us" decade.' But as the pseudonymous 'Laura Canyon' later reported in *Kerrang!*, what was going on was somewhat at odds with the ethos of 'sharing' and 'working together':

> Yes, there were acrobats. There were hot-air balloons and computer displays in giant tents dotted around the grounds. But you'd be pushing it to call it a festival. For that matter you'd be pushing it to call it 'us', what with the acts divided from the fans and each other, the police and the punters totally split ('Let's show the cops!' shouted David Lee Roth at one point when security got heavy) . . . and each of the three days divided by the genre of music, with tickets sold separately as opposed to as an overall event.[5]

The supposedly non-profit Unuson Corporation, who were in charge of the festival – and funded largely by Steve Wozniak's Apple Computer fortune – may have perceived their aim to be something akin to the spreading of brotherly love (satellites beamed pictures to the Soviet Union, apparently illustrating how technology could overcome conflict), but they had been throwing money about so recklessly (and mainly at the performers) that it wasn't long before fights began to break out over who was paid what and, indeed, the morality of accepting huge sums of cash for a single performance.[6] That is to say nothing of the fights in the crowd, stuck in the '95-degree heat, dust and humidity' of the near-desert location, as the *Los Angeles Times* reported. 'There was plenty of drug usage and scattered violence . . . and one death from an early morning fight in a parking lot.'[7]

For Joe Strummer and The Clash spokesperson and propagandist Kosmo Vinyl, in particular, there was a danger that The Clash's fee of $500,000 might make them look greedy, if not a bunch of phoneys acting against their self-declared non-materialistic values. It seemed that they were intent on making sure all this money was seen as having nothing to do with them and so they began a campaign to put the spotlight on others, particularly the Festival's organizers, whom they urged to make donations to charity. In the days and weeks before Memorial Day weekend Van Halen's fee would be reported as being $1 million, but as soon as David Bowie (appearing top of the bill on the following day) reputedly asked for $1 million-plus, the figure paid to Van Halen went up to $1.5 million without any effort on their part – simply due to the guileless Wozniak agreeing to a clause in their contract that guaranteed they would be the top-paid performer at the event. 'We never *asked* for the money', Eddie said later of the $1.5 million: 'They offered it.'[8] Wozniak and his production team were so naive in signing up bands and drawing up contracts that they had dug themselves a large black hole into which money quickly vanished, with $12 million lost mostly on overpaid band fees. Amid all this, Kosmo Vinyl – 'the loudmouth The Clash keep on their payroll to rile things up when their energies flag', in the words of *Record* magazine's John Mendelssohn – was caught muttering disparagingly about Van Halen and their 'hamburger music'.

Roth, equally able to let his mouth run off when the situation required, and possessed of the belief that one ought to live life 'as if it was the Charge of the Light Brigade – even if you are just going to brush your teeth', was never likely to leave it at that. It was perhaps something he picked up from seeing bohemian artists sling insults at each other back in Greenwich Village in the early 1960s. And so, standing atop a table with a microphone in one hand and a bottle of whisky in the other – just minutes before

Van Halen were due onstage – as the penultimate act of the day, the Scorpions, played onstage, he addressed the assembled press on the matter of the feud:

> Look, I love The Clash. I love 'Should I Stay Or Should I Go' . . . mostly because I loved [Mitch Ryder's] 'Little Latin Lupe Lu' all those years ago . . . People ask me: *what do you think of the goddam Clash criticizing you*? Well, they can't even *spell* criticism . . . but, I fully understand the Clash's position. They're trying to effect some cultural change. And they've got a new drummer to break in, man. They've got their hands full – you know what I'm sayin'?[9]

As the press lapped it up, he had one more thing to say about the money – that he needed it:

> What you need to realise is that Van Halen spends an enormous amount of money immediately after the show – on *women*. The thing The Clash don't understand is that you can't take life so goddam seriously. No one gets out *alive*. We're just here doing our usual: confusing business with pleasure.[10]

He exited with the parting words, 'it's not a question of whether you win or lose; it's how good you looked!'[11]

As John Mendelssohn wrote in a report that read more like a dispatch from some distant front line in a war zone, The Clash had taken to acting out the sentiments of their recent American hit – they agonized over the question, he noted, of 'whether they should stay or should they go'.[12] In the end they stayed – their manager Bernie Rhodes told the assembled press that 'the people out there want us to play. Besides, if we didn't play, Van Halen would call us communists.'[13] However, as The Clash biographer Marcus Gray notes, the protests about money were 'suspicious' given that they had specifically recruited a drummer for the gig – after being offered half a million dollars – and only began complaining after they discovered Van Halen were being paid more.[14]

Gray quotes The Clash guitarist Mick Jones as saying that 'we all knew that we were just doing it for the money'.[15] However, after withdrawing their threat to quit the event, The Clash took to the stage with a slew of insults directed at the audience, as Mendelssohn noted:

Once on stage, the first thing Joe Strummer did was insult his audience, in a way that demonstrated that his mastery of geography is just about equivalent to his sociopolitical acumen. 'We're here,' he croaked biliously, 'in the capital of the decadent U.S. of A.' This must have been exciting news for Devore, California.[16]

It was a performance that ended with scuffles onstage and recriminations off; between members of The Clash's entourage and the Unuson people and between Joe Strummer and Mick Jones of The Clash, who were now barely on speaking terms with each other – 'unfortunately', Mendelssohn reported of the fights, 'no one was hurt'.[17] It was guitarist Mick Jones's last performance with the band, who sacked him a few months later for deviating from the 'original spirit' of The Clash. In some places, however, this was seen as code language for the more serious crime of 'guitar hero tendencies', which may have been the result of The Clash spending the best part of a year playing stadiums in the us with The Who.

The Clash had vanished by the time Van Halen arrived at a fenced-off enclave within the Glen Helen Regional Park site to prepare for

'Look at the clothes I wear!' David Lee Roth in custom-ripped vest, pictured backstage at the Us Festival with Mark Goodman of MTV. 'Do you have your own tailor?', Goodman asked. 'Yes I do have my own tailor,' Roth replied: 'Jack the Ripper.'

their performance. The *Los Angeles Times* reported that the half-acre backstage area, which was entered via a pathway signposted 'No virgins, Journey fans or sheep allowed on trail', had been set up for a huge party for 500 guests with refrigerated food including, in the Californian tradition of exaggerated reality, 'strawberries the size of baseballs' and 'barrels of iced-down beer scattered around the enclosure'.[18] As the band enjoyed a pre-show celebration in the backstage area the audience out front were shown a film that was assumed to reveal the backstage 'preparations' as they were taking place just as the band prepared to go onstage – but it was all actually part of the show and had been partially scripted and filmed a couple of weeks before.

Via the large screens above and at the side of the stage, the audience witnessed a carnivalesque scene where actors posing as 'punk rockers, congressmen and bikers', as Roth later wrote, helped themselves to 'a Chinese buffet as big as a football field'.[19]

A local DJ, Pat 'Paraquat' Kelley of KMET, took part in proceedings to add authenticity to the idea that what the audience were watching was actually the backstage area before the show. Glamorous women – including Roth's sometime companion Sonia Braga (the Brazilian star of the Oscar-winning film *Kiss of the Spider Woman* of 1985) – canoodled with members of the band, and food fights were seen to ensue as midgets dressed in cowboy outfits rode around on saddled-up sheep, knocking over the buffet.[20] It was as if they had finally become the 'Four Stooges', orchestrating the melee.

As the film came to an end the band were ushered onstage, effecting a seamless transition. It was rather like the occasion in 1978 when the audience at Anaheim Stadium seemed to witness Van Halen parachuting into their own show – arriving onstage as they tore off flying suits and helmets. Then, too, they had been sitting backstage dressed up and ready to run onstage as the real skydivers landed behind the stage.

Roth, who was extremely drunk by this time, began the show with one of his trademark leaps into the air from Alex Van Halen's drum riser. In retrospect it was a wonder he wasn't injured. During the early part of the set, as Mendelssohn reported, the extent of the unseen partying that went on while the 'fake' party rolled on screen was evident in the fact that Roth seemed to have some trouble remaining upright. Steve Wozniak would later look back ruefully on the money he paid out on the festival, and to the sum paid to Van Halen in particular, saying that while Roth seemed pleasant enough when they met backstage before the show, he 'heard later that it was the single highest amount paid for a band' – and for what? Roth 'was practically falling down onstage. He was so drunk, slurring and forgetting lyrics and everything'[21] – as he did most nights – booze was an essential element of Van Halen's lifestyle. This wasn't business, after all – this was play. As Sylvie Simmons of *Sounds* magazine said of a performance she had witnessed in 1980 – Van Halen were 'like four drunks falling down a garbage chute'.[22] And what did some computer geek know about the niceties of rock'n'roll anyway?

The barbs against The Clash continued in a pre-show backstage interview with a hyperactive Roth – who seemed to be morphing into Lenny Bruce doing a Louis Armstrong impersonation – and were also carried onstage. In between hearty slugs taken from a whiskey bottle that was passed between Mike Anthony, Roth and one of his two midget 'bodyguards' (who was dressed as a waiter, appearing onstage between songs with a tray of Jack Daniel's Tennessee Whiskey), he addressed the audience: 'I wanna take the time to say that this is *real* whiskey here. The only people who put iced tea in Jack Daniel's bottles is *The Clash*, baby!!' Sheriff Floyd Tidwell, whose officers policed the event, accused Roth of inciting violence due to the way he would purposefully stop the performance mid-song to regale the audience with reports of their own mischief; comments that *Rolling Stone* magazine reported – and the bootleg tapes confirmed – were greeted with considerable enthusiasm from the crowd. 'More people have been arrested today *alone* than *the entire weekend* last year', he exclaimed near the beginning of the show. 'You are a bunch of rowdy motherfuckers!' Sheriff Tidwell later told a press conference that 'there are some people I'd be happy never to see back in this County again – Van Halen, for example'.[23]

Six months after the event Eddie's own thoughts on it all were somewhat laced with bitterness. 'The whole US Festival was a pain in the ass. All you hear about is how many people got killed on our day and [how much] money we made.'[24] He told Steven Rosen, perhaps implausibly, that the gig cost them more than they were reported to have made because they had to finance TV and radio specials that – buried in the small print of their contract – they never realized to be their responsibility. In exasperation,

Eddie said 'we lost more than it was ever worth. I'm still wearin'
the same pair of shoes and the same pair of pants.'[25]

And while this event was no Altamont, where violence and
murder seemed to draw the optimism of the 1960s to a close,
the Us Festival nonetheless could be seen to mark the final end
of the 1970s – even though it was already mid-1983. The way we
think of historical epochs in terms of ten-year blocks – decades –
is all wrong, especially when assessing phenomena as broad as the
'mood' of a culture, its mores and state of mind. The critic Fredric
Jameson, for instance, argues plausibly that the American 1960s
ended in 1973 with the US withdrawal from Vietnam and the end
of the optimism of that decade – underlined by the oil crisis and
Watergate scandal of 1974.[26] In rock'n'roll terms, the 1970s arguably
ends right around 1983, with the arrival of the first digital consumer
music format, the compact disc, and MTV – both of which went
mainstream in that year. The Us Festival occurred right at the time
when that phenomenon (MTV) was forcing bands to think more in
terms of video and singles. The recording of Van Halen's *MCM-
LXXXIV/1984*, indeed, was reportedly the first time that the record
company really pushed hard for the band to come up with a single
– because an MTV hit could multiply sales dramatically. It was the
first time that Warner Bros president Mo Ostin showed up in the
studio to see if the band had any hit singles on a new album.

Van Halen's rather loose performance at the Us Festival threw
up some odd moments, as if they had forgotten that there were
a couple of hundred thousand people out there in front of the
stage and they were instead back playing in some half-empty
little Hollywood club.

In between the apparently drunken renditions of their best-
known tunes, and Eddie and Alex Van Halen's frequent disappear-
ance into some zone where only they knew what they were doing,
Roth seemed at one point to have been unexpectedly abandoned

with the stage all to himself. It was as if he had momentarily become conscious of his isolation in front of all these people and, trying to fill the obvious void, began carousing with his anonymous pals in the audience ('whaddya say we go across the road and get a beer') before embarrassingly launching into some unannounced ditty. He was straining to keep it together, but the words that came out were clear enough. 'Them that's *got* shall *get*, them that's not shall lose', he sang,

> So the Bible said and it still is news
> Mama may have, papa may have
> But God bless the child that's got his own

In another life this was Billie Holiday's 'God Bless the Child', but here it delivered a momentary fall into self-revelation. Spiritually, Van Halen was that child – not an adolescent, moody and intro-spective, but a child. Just as the cover of *MCMLXXXIV/1984* and the chart-topping single 'Jump' sported the image of a winged child cheekily puffing on a cigarette, the words of 'God Bless the Child' in the mouth of Roth became a celebration of mischief.

What is it about this childlike figure – the kind found, especially, in fourteenth- and fifteenth-century Italian painting – that Roth so identified with? An echo of it appears, too, on the cover of his second solo single, 'Just a Gigolo' in 1985, where the singer is seen holding a pair of wings over his shoulder. Robert Pattison, in *The Triumph of Vulgarity*, observes it to be a droll variant on a common theme of fallen angels as vulgar heroes that reaches from William Blake's *The Marriage of Heaven and Hell* (1793) right through to rock'n'roll:

> The repressive morality of the established order will always perceive any excursion beyond its restraints as the work of Satan, and in its myths rock continually assaults these limits.

Cover of the 'Jump' single (1984), with the putto figure.

> The rocker is the fallen cherub depicted on the album cover
> of Van Halen's *1984* – Lucifer as a bad blond child with wings,
> grabbing some smokes.[27]

But perhaps he overstates the association – certainly the references
to Lucifer and Satan arise from a misinterpretation of the child
figure, which is neither fallen angel nor cherub.

Play and the importance of living in the present were Roth's
guiding principles, as he would frequently remind any interviewer
within earshot. Van Halen band members would repeat the line

'you don't *work* rock'n'roll – you *play it*' almost as if it were a mantra. What is characteristic of play, moreover, tends to be predominantly associated with childhood and adolescence. Although he was chronologically an adult, Roth organized much of his life in ways that would ensure that he did not have to be the responsible person he might have been in the adult world of work.

On the road, for instance, his travelling retinue included – for reasons of 'overall ambience', he claimed – two midget 'body-guards' named Danny and Jimmy, who had previously been clowns

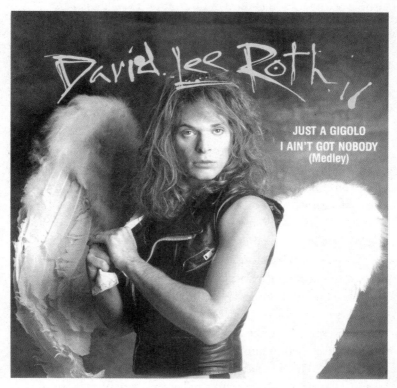

A 'winged' David Lee Roth on the cover of his second solo single, 'Just a Gigolo/I Ain't Got Nobody' (1985).

in the Ringling Bros and Barnum & Bailey Circus. For some this might have been the final proof that Roth was self-absorbed to the point of living in a fantasy world – and, in a sense, it was true. But only in the sense that rock'n'roll *was* a fantasy world come to life for those who played it. Having useless 'bodyguards' was just one more inversion of the logic and demands of the 'real' world, and represented the attention paid to detail that had a more subtle – if not to say, significant – relationship to his idea of what rock'n' roll was all about. 'When you look out of your bedroom door and a midget goes by in a bath towel, you know you're not in life insurance', he told Mick Brown of London's *Sunday Times*:

> And it's important for me to keep reminding myself, to keep populating this little world and adding to it. I was always disappointed when I was a little kid, when I found out that other people were faking me out – they didn't really dress like that, or look like that or behave like that off stage.[28]

As a member of the Van Halen crew told a *Rolling Stone* writer in 1984, Roth's retreat from the adult world was nearly absolute: 'We're *all* childish, but Dave hasn't been born yet.' When the interviewer posed this observation to Roth he didn't deny it: 'People tell me I live in my own little world. I tell them, "Well, at least they know me there."'[29]

Yet aside from his clear identification with a world of playful possibilities normally associated with being young, there is a second, more interesting explanation for the *MCMLXXXIV/1984* album's front cover image. It wasn't just the image of *any* child, but a representation that was rendered in the form of an homage to the style and content of the allegorical painting of the Italian Renaissance. This winged child figure – often taken for a cherub or an angel – conforms, rather, to similar representations identified by the term 'putti' ('putto' in the singular). During the Renaissance these child figures had been revived from the kind of winged infants that had earlier appeared on sarcophagi in Roman antiquity. But, in the fourteenth- and fifteenth-century context, these putti functioned as figures of deep ambiguity – much like trickster figures, you might say. For instance, where a cherub is taken as simply a childlike angel (a messenger and servant of God, and the fallen angel is the servant of Lucifer) the putto, by contrast, represents something more complicated – a kind of unadulterated and unpredictable spirit.

The contexts in which these putti appear, and the meanings attached to them, reveal that they form part of a broader category of the fantastic, as experienced, for instance, in allegorical dreams and visions. They are also termed 'spiritelli' or 'sprites' – meaning *pure spirit* – driven by feeling, sensation and, above all, the urge to play. Among the many qualities to be associated with them are cunning, charm and the 'sheer joy of infancy'. Charles Dempsey, in his book *Inventing the Renaissance Putto*, has noted that

> putti embodied a minor species of demon, in their nature neither good nor bad . . . They included natural spirits, animal spirits, and the spirits of sight and sound, as well as hobgoblin fantasies, bogeys, and the spirits contained in wine. Among the sensations ascribed to spiritelli were feelings of love, erotic arousal, and startling frights.[30]

These infant sprites are in keeping with Roth's view of rock-'n'roll and the inspiration he drew from Zen ideas – 'childlikeness must be restored', Suzuki wrote – and they represent a lack of self-consciousness and the childlike tendency to give in to impulses that 'affect the body without conscious bidding, unwilled by the intellect'.[31] It is such a tendency that lies at the root of most of Roth's lyrical concerns. In 'Jump', for instance, the switch from the self-doubting sentiments of the verses to the recklessness of the chorus – *go ahead and do it, jump* – might be seen as Roth's inner putti taking over to resolve a dilemma.

With sessions for the *MCMLXXXIV/1984* album taking place at Eddie's new studio, which he had named 5150 – a police radio call number that, translated roughly, meant something like 'madman on the loose' – Roth and Ted Templeman, in particular, had to adjust to new recording conditions, and a new attitude to time and work. The first song to be cut at the studio was 'Jump', a song that Eddie had been trying to get the band to record for a couple of years. The fact that he had now managed to achieve this would signal that he was finally gaining more control of the band.

Yet although the song 'Jump' would become Van Halen's biggest hit, it was met with resistance from within and it almost never saw the light of day. While Eddie would speak often about 'his songs' there was a lot more to the process of how Van Halen created their music. At the time, the band's publishing was split four ways, with each member credited as co-songwriter, but the truth was that the songs (considered as words and music) were principally co-creations of the singer and the guitarist. Eddie came up with the musical parts – riffs, chord structures, as well as fully formed and complete pieces of music – which the whole band might then work on, suggesting that parts of riffs or chord structures could be re-arranged one way and another until verses and choruses took shape as the foundation for what would ultimately become completed songs. This process of almost collective editing among the band and production team worked for a long time because, as Roth told Steven Rosen, they had respect for each others' ears and for the collective sense of what the band should be achieving in the studio:

> You never hear anyone say 'what the hell do you know about playing the drums', or 'what the hell do you know about

singing', 'cos, you know, none of us really knew for sure –
about anything.[32]

But in terms of how the creative process unfolded, it is clear that
Eddie provided the initial spark of the music that Roth needed
to work off, and to which he could add words and vocal melodies
which, as with the music, the rest of the band and Templeman
might then work on, knocking it all into shape. As Eddie noted
in an interview in 1985, the vocal melodies, which bore the stamp
of Roth's peculiar amalgam of non-rock influences (as well as
being vehicles for the words he wrote), constituted essentially
half the songs:

> I never say [to Dave] 'Here's the music. Here's the melody. Fit
> words to these notes.' Because that would be really ridiculous
> . . . Dave has done some stuff with the music that has been
> handed to him that has blown me away.[33]

What was at stake with 'Jump' went far beyond disquiet over
the course of the band's normal song selection process for Eddie
– he felt strongly about the tune but he sensed that Roth did not
want to add his input to it in order to work it up into a song the
band could cut. The whole affair seemed to him to demonstrate
a kind of musical censorship, with others determined to box him
into an unwanted role as merely some kind of guitar-slinger. The
extent to which this annoyed Eddie is clear in the fact that when-
ever critics would try and define him as solely a guitar player, he
would, somewhat disingenuously, claim that in fact guitar was
only his *fourth* instrument. 'You haven't heard all my music', he
told Charles M. Young of *Musician*. 'Nobody knows what I do.
They've only seen the one of me which is Van Halen [the band].'
On the brink of Roth's departure from the band, in late 1984,
Eddie joked that if he ever made a solo album it would consist

of tunes featuring the other instruments he either played or had dabbled in: saxophone, piano and cello – 'I'd call it *Guitar: What Guitar?*'[34]

Eventually, however, with the help of engineer, Donn Landee, and in virtue of owning the studio where the band now worked, Eddie kept the others – Roth and Templeman particularly – at bay, and presented them with a demo of 'Jump' that was more worked out than the original idea that he had kept in his bag of tapes for the previous year or so.

According to Templeman, once they decided to go for it, the song was re-recorded from the template laid down in this newer demo in one day – music and vocals. Roth took a tape with the instrumental track and disappeared to work on the lyrics and vocal melody in his own peculiar fashion, which just happened to involve being driven around the Los Angeles canyons and along the Coast Highway by Larry Hostler, his roadie, as he revealed to *Melody Maker*:

> We get into the 1951 low-rider Mercury painted bright orange and red with a white pin-stripe down the middle, Larry drives and I sit in the back . . . and I write the songs. We play the tape over and over again on the stereo and about every hour-and-a-half I lean over and go 'Say, Lar, what d'you think of this?'[35]

This was another one of those tales that neatly allowed Roth to put the result down to a chance combination of factors beyond his control: 'I guess that means Larry is primarily responsible for what you hear.'[36]

'Jump', in addition to what has been said above, is also in keeping with the stress Roth and Van Halen placed on *the now* – that Zen Californian condition of enlightenment. But more than that it works because the words and the sentiment do match the *feel* of the music: as Roth's words reach the point of anticipating the leap into the unknown – as he sings 'can't you see me standing here I got my back against the record machine' – Eddie, with a tastefully chosen guitar lick, and Alex, complementing him on cymbals, actually give the sense, like the title of the song itself, of becoming groundless; of being lifted up by a gust of air or, again, surfing a wave – the musical bridge section sparkles and glistens like the spindrift of breaking surf in bright sunshine. 'Jump' seems, in that respect, one of the most perfectly Zen Californian of Van Halen's creations.

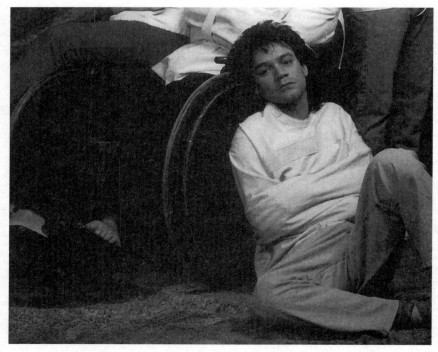

Eddie Van Halen appearing – not for the first time – in a straitjacket; this time on the sleeve of the first single released by the band post-Roth, and recorded in his Hollywood Hills studio, which he named '5150'– the Californian police code used to indicate an escaped psychiatric patient.

9 SAIL TO THE MOON

It is not only in dreams, or in that mild delirium which precedes sleep, but it is even awakened when I hear music – that perception of an analogy and an intimate connexion between colours, sounds and perfumes. It makes me fall into a deep reverie.

– E.T.A. Hoffmann

If David Lee Roth gave himself over to feeling, it was all in pursuit of a Zen-like ambiguity. Not seeking to control or adulterate his impulses was his way of being in a position where he could exploit reality, whatever configuration it might take. But if Roth revelled in ambiguity, it was as nothing compared to the enigma that seemed to envelop Eddie Van Halen as the years passed.

Eddie, certainly later in his career, gave the impression of a man who had been to the moon and subsequently lost all means of communicating an experience – an existence – that he could no longer truly make sense of himself. Like Brian Wilson of The Beach Boys, who simply vanished under the weight of creative pressure for a decade or more, Eddie's talent seems to have stripped him bare, left him at the mercy of feeling (where Roth more enthusiastically embraced it). As recently as 2006, almost ten years after he had last released new music, he would say that he had recorded enough material to release a dozen albums. However, he wasn't releasing it. Whereas Roth, at the height of Van Halen's success, became like the wave he was riding, Eddie seemed to be engulfed by one, and cast adrift by it. As a musician, he was not alone in displaying a certain kind of receptivity to sensation. To submit to being pulled in by something that constituted a much greater force than he was on his own seemed to show respect for the unknowns of musical creativity. 'I'm just a medium', he told *Musician* in 1991:

The shit's coming from somewhere. I don't sit down and really think. I just get in this mode and I do what I *do*. That's why I hate doing interviews because people ask me, 'how do you do what you do?' I don't know!'[1]

The thing for Eddie was that what began with the merely audible – with the sound of music – extended to the other senses. This was what complicated the matter, and made it difficult to communicate, making Eddie feel as though 'there's somebody up there pullin' the strings for me'.[2]

When The Beach Boys' Brian Wilson recorded 'Good Vibrations' – *vibes*, or vibrations, being mainly associated with feeling good or bad – it is not surprising that he had fallen under the sway of a mixture of 1960s California esoterica: 'astrology, Tantric Buddhism, numerology, acid mysticism' and so on.[3] For Eddie, the way that music took on its vibe-like quality was somewhat less to do with taking a trip through the spiritual supermarket, as many thought Brian Wilson was doing in those years, and more bound to the fact that strong sensory perceptions seemed to deliver the music as almost a narcotic. It hit him like a drug, knocked him into that kind of 'time out of time' associated with states of ecstasy.

Eddie was synaesthetic. Accounts of the condition go back at least to the eighteenth century and it has been associated, in particular, with Romantic writers and musicians ever since – Romanticism being an important predecessor of rock music when we bear in mind that its chief characteristic was the elevation of feeling to the greatest human good.[4]

As Jeremy Strick has written in *Visual Music* (2005), 'synaesthetic associations were thought to result from a heightened state of aesthetic awareness', a receptiveness to emotion, feeling and to the aspects of one's world, such as art and music, that reflected those very qualities.[5] The Romantic artists sought the Sublime through all kinds of sensory immersion, and the fascination of the synaesthetic is something captured by the nineteenth-century French writer Charles Baudelaire's poem 'Correspondences':

> Long-held echoes, blending somewhere else
> into one deep and shadowy unison
> as limitless as darkness and as day,
> the sounds, the scents, the colors correspond.[6]

For those touched, like Baudelaire, by synaesthesia, more than one of the senses are often involved, not just the hearing-sense and how that relates to colour (as is common among most synaesthetes). However, hearing is particularly important because it opens the individual up to a mysterious and enchanting world that is elusive and, therefore, 'music held a special place as a referent or inspiration for such heightened states'.[7] Music's 'non-mimetic' dimensions – that is to say, the fact that it is pure sensation – also means that the musician seems, in the words of John Hamilton, to be other than a normal 'cognitive subject'; which is all to say that we should not be surprised if musicians are a bit odd. As a result of the way music can lure a performer into the condition of self-loss, of appearing to be played *by* the music and not the other way around, it is, and has always been, associated with madness.[8]

For Eddie Van Halen the guitar player, the *experience* of tone and feeling were fundamental to his pursuit of inspiration. In his mind's eye he knew the music was good if it was 'brown'. In fact, his brother Alex shared in this – the same colour, he said, might also describe his snare drum tone. But it seemed that this description wasn't just a way to approximate – in language – something that could not be adequately expressed in any other way. As Alex told one journalist: 'I don't compare it to brown – it *is* brown.'[9] Eddie's 'brown' sound, as we will see, went arguably deeper and straight to the root of how he connected to the world. And, like other synaesthetes, he experienced these sensory correspondences when he was in a meditative or ecstatic state – meaning that the association of feeling with colour was the result of more than sound alone.

While sound – musical sound – is the means through which the 'brown' manifests itself, Eddie has also described it in terms of a number of other qualities and sensory correspondences: it is variously 'warm', 'sweet', 'fat' or 'thick', 'wood'-like, as well as 'buttery' and 'meaty'. 'The brown,' Eddie mused enigmatically to Charles Young of *Musician* magazine in 1984, 'I am into the brown. Most people cannot understand the brown, can't put a finger on it, but it affects them subliminally.'[10]

If this all seems a bit unhinged from reality, it was something Eddie seemed to play up to. Apart from the name of the studio, 5150, he also appeared in a video for Van Halen's song 'Hot for Teacher' wearing a straitjacket and looking like an extra from *One Flew Over the Cuckoo's Nest*. When speaking to interviewers he described himself as 'a sick fuck', a 'geek' and so on. In a *Rolling Stone* profile in 1984 by Debby Miller, a member of the band's entourage told her that Eddie was a dear soul, but was so 'out there' as to be 'on the Moon'.[11]

However, concerns about his grip on reality aside, there was a sonic, or musical, consistency evident in the work that he thought was 'brown'. As far back as Van Halen's debut album in 1978, and through the changes in his tone, there was something in the ambience that connected the later examples of this brown sound – thick and fat – to the somewhat brighter guitar tones evident on that first album. This is the sense of air. It is heard also in the synthesized electronic swells of the instrumental '1984' and 'Jump' – the track it segues into – which both feel more natural and organic than the often more mechanical sound of the synthesizer in popular music. The chords of 'Jump', for instance, have a The

Who-like stamp about them, but they aren't clipped in the kind of way one suspects they could have been in the hands of Pete Townshend; instead they *breathe* and *expire*. On MCMLXXXIV/1984, this sense of air is also found in the guitar work, as Eddie seems to approximate the tones and dextrous flourishes of a host of wind instruments – particularly sax and clarinet, but also trumpet – as he moves around the neck of his guitar.

Additionally, the 'rhythm' parts he plays differentiate him from other guitarists, and illustrate a highly developed and individualistic style that is largely determined by the use of the hands and fingers in ways that extended the vocabulary of guitar – he damps, slaps, taps, rubs and mutes the strings with his hands. With his pick he slides, scrapes and digs on them to create a variety of sound effects that fill out the sonic space. Often he scrapes or picks out notes and ringing harmonics under the main figure or riff – it can be heard in the song 'Panama', in which his playing sounds fairly relaxed and easy, but the hands are casually working all the time. The tremolo bar, traditionally used for vibrato, is employed not only to bend notes and produce dive-bombing descents, but also – as in 'House of Pain' – giant chordal shifts that give a sense of the tectonic, of the earth moving beneath the band, who seem to sway, disorientated and cut adrift from any secure grounding.

These aspects of Van Halen's aesthetics of feeling get lost in discussions of mere technique – they are more to do with adding depth and colour to the musical picture than they are to do with flash, and are what allows that one guitar, often with no overdubs, to define so completely the sonic landscape. The light touch of hands gives an airy and spatial quality to the guitar on 'Girl Gone Bad' (from MCMLXXXIV/1984), a tune that recalls the feel of Cream's smacked-out, sweltering, 'Dance the Night Away'. Here the instrumental interplay creates a turbulence, a circulatory motion, that sees guitar and drums move around, and in and out, and on top of each other to create something akin to an extra autonomous layer of sound that the players have little control over. It seems nothing like the 4/4 of hard rock.

Quite often the timbre or tone achieved is reminiscent of a saxophone. In fact, Eddie once admitted that the reason he fell for Eric Clapton's playing of the mid- to late 1960s was that it reminded him of that instrument, which he had originally intended to learn before guitar. 'I love sax', he told Steve Rosen. 'Guitar is actually kinda like sax – like some of the old Cream guitar tones.'[12] Once that correspondence between a certain tonal quality and particular instruments has been planted in the mind, it can soon enough be heard everywhere in Clapton's playing with Cream. His guitar solo on the studio version of 'I'm So Glad' provides a good example. It actually sounds like – has the form of – a sax break; similarly the honking riff on 'Strange Brew' from their *Disraeli Gears* (1967) album is very much the kind of riff that a sax player – or two of them playing together off each other – might produce. With that idea of the relationship of the wind instrument to guitar, listen to some of Eddie's upper range lead lines, where the sound seems to move into the tone range of clarinet – those fluid tapped-out notes on the solo for 'Jump' (between 2:16 and 2:30), for instance. There seems to be no other adequate comparison. And when he taps out or picks harmonics – at the beginning of 'Girl Gone Bad' and 'Top Jimmy' – they are reminiscent of patterns and tones heard in bebop trumpet. But all the time, there is a sense of *air*, of breathing.

When Eddie listened to those Cream records, often slowed to 16rpm on his record player, he may have sensed someone achieving with the guitar the kind of articulation that a sax player had available to them, because what the instrument was actually articulating was a human being breathing through it. That sense seems to be what he took from Eric Clapton, the need for a kind of physical engagement with the music, if a way could be found, that might produce something that could be *felt* as much as it was heard. In performance Eddie seemed often to seek the gust of air that might carry him away. He could get lost in 'whirring and whirling, bending and bleeding splays of notes', as Barney Hoskyns once wrote, playing rock'n'roll, but 'like a John Coltrane'.[13]

Eddie's ability to play with air was the result of many years of experimentation on the so-called 'brown' and the creation of a bastardized guitar, comprised of materials and components of several different types of that instrument, which observers called a 'Frankenstrat' (after *Strato*caster, whose body shape it borrowed, and Frankenstein's monster, who was made up of scraps). It is perhaps no accident that he felt able to experiment and modify what for others was equipment that they just accepted as it was. Southern California – Los Angeles, in particular – was home to the hot rod; which is to say, to the idea of the car itself as an expression of the fantastic and excessive. The kind of attitude associated with hot rod culture, though, seemed be something that people simply 'inhaled', that was everywhere. As Reyner Banham wrote in 1971, the hot rod was 'almost as specific to the Los Angeles freeways as the surf-board is to the Los Angeles beaches'.[14] It sprung from 'delinquent origins' and resulted in 'wonders wrought in backyards by high-school dropouts upon domestic Detroit-built machines', which saw run of the mill cars transformed into 'wild extravaganzas of richly coloured and exotically shaped metal'.[15]

What Eddie Van Halen did to the guitar was essentially of this order – he took a standardized object, ripped it apart, and fine-tuned it to produce something new that elevated the homemade into an art form. It was out of proportion with the norm, exaggerated, comprised of apparently incompatible parts, but as squarely in keeping with the Californian pursuit of self-invention as were those hot rods or, indeed, the 'deconstructed' appearance of architect Frank Gehry's infamous Santa Monica house. These were all creations that seemed to express a sense of that place, Los Angeles and Southern California, and a can-do state of mind that had always separated itself from history and tradition.

Van Halen's sought-after 'brown' sound – particularly the quality of warmth – rested on the matter of how to make an electric guitar *hum* and blow at high volume without generating screeching feedback or the sharpness of tone achieved with a fuzz pedal. Sax, clarinet and other wind instrument players, for instance, could achieve and modulate the attack and decay of notes by the use of breath – and breathing, of course, could be very subtle. Blowing *through* the notes, a wind player's two hands were free to manipulate the sound that air – breathing – first begins to articulate. But pushing air seemed not to be a quality of musical articulation as easily available to a guitarist; rather, a guitar player's sustain came more obviously via the means of hands and electricity, which is to say, through the bending of notes and the use of vibrato and the ways that the sound could be enlarged through amplification. What Eddie did was to figure out how to become a kind of conduit for electrical currents that just seemed to blow through him, through that overdriven guitar, slapped together from scraps.

Into the early days of Van Halen's recording career, the warm – 'brown' – glow of electricity was fed into amplifiers whose tube valves, due to Eddie's hot-rodding modifications, would literally *melt* as he played through them. This was because he had altered the voltage feed to the equipment using a domestic light dimmer switch control. By reducing the power input to the amplifier by 'dimming' down he was then able to crank it to maximum output but without losing tone, and without generating feedback and distortion. The only problem this created was in those melting valves, which had to be replaced daily at some expense during touring. Ultimately the unique tonal quality achieved on *Van*

Halen (1978) could not be maintained because it meant destroying equipment in the act of creation.

One other important modification that helped to achieve this rich and warm, non-fuzzy, 'brown' tone was to the pick-ups – whose magnetic poles, resting under the strings, amplified the acoustic string sound, carrying it through coils that vibrated in response to the guitarist's plucking and strumming and into the amplifier. Seeking a way to cut out buzzing, distortion and feedback while still being able to play at high volume, Eddie built his own pick-ups from a combination of single-coil (Stratocaster) and Humbucking (Gibson) parts, which were slapped together haphazardly with only his judicious eye to measure the steps in the experimental process. Perhaps because this was California, and Eddie saw himself as 'just a punk kid trying to get a sound out of a guitar' that he couldn't buy, he thought that the kind of wax surfers used to smooth out their boards, paraffin wax, might also help smooth out his sound, make it more 'brown'.[16] Thus he would heat up a can of the wax and drop the pick-ups in until he thought they had absorbed enough of the liquid so that the wire coils would cease vibrating (and thus the kind of buzzing that came with high volume would also cease) once the wax had solidified. Then, rather unorthodoxly, these homemade pick-ups would be drilled tight into the wood rather than floating on springs, as was the case with any off-the-rack guitar. This was because, as Eddie told one interviewer, 'everything has to be connected . . . the wood is where the sustain comes from.'[17]

Long before the band had made it, Eddie seemed to be aware that the guitar parts, the neck and the body, and the wood these were sourced from also held another important key to the warm sound he wanted. He built and destroyed many guitars trying to figure out how certain types of wood would help produce the kind of tone he needed, all the while paying attention to the kind

of details with which only an obsessive experimenter would bother
– not only the thickness of a cut of wood, for instance, but its
density (taking a saw to it, which he would do, was a sure way of
finding out about that). All of that, of course, is not to mention
the specifics of how the other parts – the electrical components,
the metal parts of the bridge and the tremolo – were attached
to the body of the guitar and how they performed under duress.
A long period of trial and error led Eddie to place a great deal of
emphasis on knowing which woods were best for tone and which
were not. For instance, Fender Stratocasters – in addition to having
thinner sounding single-coil pick-ups – were made of a type of
wood called alder, which he thought was cheap, and therefore
as significant as the pick-ups in producing the guitar's signature
'thin' sound – a sound he didn't want.

What he discovered through long periods of experimentation
was that the wood of his favoured guitar body had to be heavy and
often thicker than normal, and sourced from wood taken from a
korina (an African tree). He used a Stratocaster-shaped body – for
aesthetic reasons – but it was specially made to get the thickness
required. Also important were untreated fingerboards; that is,
just bare un-lacquered wood on the neck of the guitars because,
he told one interviewer, 'I like to feel the wood.'[18] The wood, of
course, was *brown*.

Eddie's musical obsessiveness was clearly related to his loner
temperament, and as much as anything else gave him the aura
of someone spaced out to the extent that they saw the world in a
way that couldn't be anything but idiosyncratic. But, it was always
about the synaesthetic aspects of sound and tone, about unmediated *feeling* as the source of music. 'There are too many people on
this basketball that's floating around the sun, who are too afraid
to allow themselves to feel', Eddie mused to *Rolling Stone*'s Debby
Miller.[19] In many ways he was a living embodiment of someone

Eddie Van Halen, 1978, with the first widely seen version of his home-built 'hot rod' guitar. Its uniqueness was partly to do with the wood of its construction, and his modified pick-ups. 'The thing I do to the pick-ups is pot 'em in paraffin wax – surfboard wax – which cuts out the high, obnoxious feedback.'

who could not help but just *be*, in an almost unmediated sense, in a kind of way that put him 'on the Moon'. As Charles M. Young observed, there was 'something eerie about Eddie Van Halèn, almost holy, Michael Jacksonly':

> The guy has *no* persona, no wall of normal behaviour between him and his suspicious world. Just pure essence of feeling. When he likes you, he kisses you. When he's frustrated, he throws one of his delicate hands into the wall and busts a knuckle. It would appear to be the only route to the Brown sound.[20]

When *Melody Maker*'s Steve Sutherland met Eddie in 1984 it was also with busted knuckles *and* toes after giving a bad show: 'he grabs my hand and shakes it heartily,' Sutherland wrote, 'his blood staining my palm'. 'Music is nothing but a feeling', Eddie told the journalist: 'I'm not trying to prove *shit*. I just hope people *feel* something.' His wife had apparently talked him into using his feet instead of his hands to release his frustration, but – he said – 'I broke three toes, so I went back to my hands . . . at least until my foot heals'.[21] Sutherland's encounter with Eddie was enough to locate the guitarist in the ranks of rock music's oddballs. Some time after the interview was published, in April 1984, *Melody Maker* drew up a list of rock'n'roll's 'Top Ten Fruitcakes'. And there, at number six, was Eddie, along with more well-known loonies like Brian Wilson (number one), Roky Erickson (number two), Julian Cope (number seven) and Syd Barrett (a surely disappointing number nine).[22] Yet like many of those so-called fruitcakes who exist in the public mind as manifestations of the tortured artist so beloved of Romanticism, their very being was defined by a connection to something that carried them off to another place – whether it was madness, drugs or maintaining a childlike connection to the world – that was then channelled into the music they made.

This inability to put the world at a distance, which this 'madness' implies, brings us back to the issue of synaesthesia which, we should remember, usually involves music's relationship to all kinds of other modalities of the sensual. For centuries it was thought that 'sounds acted as ciphers of the universe'; and notable composers and musicians had long thought of sounds in terms of colour.[23] In the twentieth century, for instance, figures such as Alexander Scriabin, Olivier Messiaen and Arnold Schoenberg, to name a few, thought of their music precisely in such terms, and often to the bemusement of others. As the music historian Olivia Mattis has written, the correspondence of sound to colour is an important element of what allows us to make sense of music, whether we are aware of it or not:

> Tone color, or timbre, is one of sound's five parameters; the others are pitch, volume, duration, and envelope (the attack and decay of a sound). Tone color is the aspect of sound that allows the listener to differentiate, say, a violin from a clarinet.[24]

As a guitarist in a rock'n'roll band one of Eddie's motivations in pursuing the 'brown', as we have seen, was to be able to play at high volumes without losing tonal warmth. Famously, his main guitar between 1977 and the mid-1980s was unique in having only one pick-up and one control knob – most guitars had at least two pick-ups and three to five control knobs. This new streamlined look of Eddie's was copied by dozens of guitar manufacturers in the 1980s in order to sell guitars that looked like a Van Halen model. But on his famous 'Frankenstrat' guitar – originally painted with black and white stripes on the cover of *Van Halen* – while the control knob did indeed turn up the volume, it read 'tone'. In other words: louder, for Eddie, just meant greater *tone*.

But tone, like colour, is understood to exist on a spectrum. As Douglas Kahn has written 'the most generalized synaesthetic schemes' always revolve around the duality of 'dark color/low tone and light color/high tone'. Light and colour, of course, are what constitute the visual field, allowing us to discern objects and forms and, as such, are concerned with seeing. But for the synaesthetic, the ear and the eye come together. An eighteenth-century composer named André Grétry suggested that to the ear, extremes of tone were best understood in visual terms: 'Lowered or flattened tones have the same effect on the ear as dark, gloomy colours on the eye; the raised or sharpened tones have, on the contrary, an effect similar to that of lively bright colors.'[25]

Eddie's favoured tone, as we have seen was a deep, rich and warm tone – hence it was 'brown', and this is what distinguished him from other guitar players. The sound often favoured by many heavy metal guitarists, in particular, seemed to him to be like 'razor blades coming at your ears'.[26] It was a description that contrasted the sharp metallic grate of an amplifier pushed to feedback level with the more rounded-out, flat and soft sound of, say, a soprano saxophone – a sound that expanded in space rather than cutting it up. Because this 'brown' sound is so connected to feeling and sensation (and not just to the technical details of what produces it as an auditory phenomenon), its peculiarities – and how it relates to Eddie Van Halen as a person – lie also in the way that other non-musical aspects end up contributing to how it might be encountered.

Eddie got this 'brown' feeling after transporting himself into a state where musical ideas seemed to freely flow through him from some unknown source. 'In order to come up with anything different, a tune or whatever, I gotta sit totally in silence by myself, playing my guitar for about two or three hours', he said. 'It's almost like meditating.'[27] And, importantly, the way into this meditative state was followed always with the help of alcohol. It became well known in later years that he was a drinker of some repute. In a *Rolling Stone* cover story and interview from 1995 – during one of Eddie's post-recording bouts of sobriety – the reporter David Wild recounted stopping at a liquor store on the Sunset Strip to buy a soda as he made his way to Eddie's house, only to be confronted with a photograph of the guitarist above the store entrance: 'a giant blow-up of a hammered looking Eddie Van Halen between similar photos of Keith Moon and Liberace' in a makeshift gallery of the store's celebrity visitors over the years.[28]

But his so-called 'struggle' with alcohol really masks the complexities of artistic creativity, if not the reality of who Eddie was as a musician; which is to say, there is a sense in which if the alcohol was taken out of the equation, he would have never reached the meditative state where inspiration flowed. Musicians – especially those who are enraptured by the feelings that sound produces – have, historically, often relied heavily on alcohol and drugs. In jazz, as in rock'n'roll, where the musician's singularity was thought to be expressed chiefly through communion with an instrument (particularly in trumpet and sax players), drugs and alcohol use was common. As Geoff Dyer notes, 'the likes of Coleman Hawkins and Lester Young who dominated jazz in the 1930s ended up as alcoholics', while later generations submitted to 'a virtual epidemic of heroin addiction': 'Many cleaned up eventually . . . but the list of those who were never addicted would make up a far less impressive roster of talent than those who were.'[29]

Eddie knew it, too. During a live radio interview in 2006 when he was asked why Eric Clapton had so inspired him, Eddie declared his preference for the strung-out, alcohol- and heroin-addicted Clapton over the clean and sober musician he became in the 1980s and beyond. 'He's trying to be B. B. King now', Eddie said. 'But B. B. King does it better. I hate to say it,' he observed, 'but he was better when he was a heroin addict.'[30] He thought Clapton played better because the heroin (and booze) was obviously a very big part of what enabled him to be transported *through* the music. And, in this respect, Clapton himself had made no attempt to

Eddie Van Halen takes flight, 1982. Here, he is pulling the kind of shapes that were more commonly seen in the concrete bowls that skateboarders would carve in Southern Californian backyards.

hide the fact that he took his cue from predecessors in jazz and blues like Charlie Parker and Robert Johnson, if not from the romanticism of addiction. It is no surprise, then, that Clapton – along with a few others – was among the first musicians to emerge from rock'n'roll and acquire the same kind of aura as jazz musicians, particularly trumpet and saxophone players. Most of the rest of those who attained a similar aura, all guitarists – Jimmy Page, Jimi Hendrix and Pete Townshend, for instance – gave into heroin, and alcohol, as well.[31]

All of Eddie's quirks and idiosyncrasies – from the obsession with wood to the necessity of alcohol – went directly into making him the musician he was. In particular, they related to the amount of time he gave to the music, which was time spent precisely *not* growing up. 'It doesn't even matter whether there are people out there or not', he told Steve Sutherland of *Melody Maker* in 1984:

> Because I actually get off more when I'm sitting on the floor in my hotel room, totally drunk, smoking a cigarette and getting in that state of mind where it's like meditating – just sitting there for hours playing. I start floating and things just come out.[32]

At the end of their meeting Sutherland described a roadie entering the hotel room they were using for the interview with a selection of strong spirits, and Eddie almost indiscriminately picking a bottle of vodka, and saying 'uh, I'll take that one . . . it's bigger.'[33] On the road, this is what he did almost every night – took out his tape machine and plied himself with booze to raise to life the music. 'I want to play when I'm drunk', he told David Wild in 1995. 'I have such an association between the two.'[34] And during recording he would typically drink from early in the day until late at night, all the time trying to maintain the warm glow that alcohol produced, and which then became so associated with the sweet and warm tone that he identified as the 'brown' that it was almost impossible to break the habit without giving up on music.

The mystery of the 'brown' is that Eddie found it when he had divested himself of his inhibitions and opened his senses to the flow of the unconscious. It's why he would say, without being disingenuous, that he didn't know where the music came from. 'Ninety percent of what I came up with, I don't know where the hell it comes from.'[35] The 'brown' being a connection to unconscious or semi-conscious states was evident in the fact, as he told one magazine, that he would find himself receiving all sorts of music, 'all sorts of shit', as he lay in bed, in that woozy delirium that precedes sleep – 'just as I start to drift off'.[36]

Sail to the moon.

Eddie Van Halen, 1985. 'Everyone says he's a nice guy, and that's exactly how he comes across: friendly, polite, soft-spoken and ill at ease only when the conversation turns to his musical skills. Unlike most musicians, he's more comfortable discussing his personal life than discussing his music.'

'The Unabomber' and 'Colonel Gaddafi' in Detroit, 1978, enjoy some downtime together in the days when they still shared a common goal.

10 WIPEOUT, c. 1984–2007

In reality, as a fundamental physical feat, surfing on a wave is
a phenomenal conjunction of forces; the mathematics of it are
profoundly complex.

– Drew Kampion, *The Lost Coast*

The effortlessness of Van Halen's first six years as a recording band
– with six albums recorded in a period that was, cumulatively,
probably no more than two to three months' worth of studio
time – ended up being killed by time itself: by the crawling,
clawing hands of the clock which, by 1983, had a hold of them.
In decamping to the Hollywood hills, Eddie Van Halen had put
on the brakes, perhaps in recognition of the fact that, as W. T.
Lhamon said of too much living in the moment, 'Unregulated
energy, like any explosion, soon expends itself.'[1]

Van Halen's desire to give themselves over to the moment
had found them coasting upon the momentum of a wave that
they themselves, as a single entity, had become. As is the case
with the surfer, however, as soon as self-consciousness emerges,
the possibility of faltering begins to dominate the thought process.
Circumstances precipitated by Eddie finally gaining control of his
band in 1983 forced the band to work – and the problem was that
work was the antithesis of Van Halen's very being up to that point.

In his studio, Eddie was oblivious to the demands of others.
Recording *MCMLXXXIV/1984* he was determined to take his time
and work on the music as it came, rather than reverting to the
old 'fast'n'dirty' approach that had worked so well in the past.
And it was the unpredictable nature of Eddie's working methods
that would start to become too much for David Lee Roth to bear.
Although members of the band would later claim that the total

amount of time spent recording this final album with Roth was relatively short – perhaps four weeks – it was nonetheless a protracted affair that involved being in and out of the studio a lot, and not getting things done quickly.

For a month or so during the summer of 1983 Eddie was shut away in a beach house in Malibu, a time during which he was preoccupied with work on the soundtrack for a TV movie that starred his wife, Valerie Bertinelli. During many days of musical experimentation – much to the horror of the owner of the house, the schmaltzy composer Marvin Hamlisch – Eddie all but destroyed the white grand piano that came with the rental deal, taking a saw to it and clogging up its insides with a variety of kitchen implements to create a John Cage-ish prepared piano effect. Around this time Eddie would also enjoy pulling out tapes of this music to show how 'fucked-up' he really was when given free reign.[2] Only a minute or so of this would surface some thirteen years later on the post-Roth album, *Balance* (1996). But it was this growing trend towards outside and non-band projects that left Roth feeling that the guitarist was set on sabotaging the band. 'Ed Van Halen', he said some years later, 'the Unabomber'.

At times, the making of the *MCMLXXXIV/1984* album degenerated into a stand-off between Eddie and Donn Landee on one side and Roth and Ted Templeman on the other, involving – Roth said – 'the type of ludicrous behaviour where I'm sitting with the producer in one studio in Hollywood, while Ed and the engineer are in another studio'.[3] Eddie, Landee and drummer Alex had, to some extent, formed an autonomous working unit and carried on recording material for the album on their own. However, Eddie and Landee, especially, were 'working all night, not getting up during the day', Roth said, and 'threatening to burn the master tapes' if he and Templeman didn't stop making demands about how things ought to be done. 'It turned into a lot of alcohol-fuelled wasted time', he added.[4]

The sessions for this last album saw the band 'at each other's throats more than ever', the singer said. Yet this in itself wasn't a problem – it could in fact be conducive to good results, but only if things were allowed to develop, to take on their own configuration. The conflict provided something to play with: 'The best accomplishments are not achieved when everybody is sitting around going, you're great! Do you think I'm great, too? You do? Great!'[5] However, where Roth thought that out of conflict could come 'marvellous, competitive, flame-throwing, hallelujah, dump truck size, Bubba's hot barbecue', Eddie could no longer deal with his singer, whom he would soon be comparing to notorious dictators like Idi Amin and Colonel Gaddafi.[6]

And so the recording of *MCMLXXXIV/1984* in the Hollywood hills was the beginning of the end of an association that began in Pasadena ten years before, in 1973. The making of the album also effectively ended the long-running partnership of Templeman and Landee. Landee, Eddie's closest friend for some time, continued to work with Van Halen for another two albums but he and Templeman would never work together again. 'You can wonder what Roth and Eddie Van Halen are doing in the same band', Charles Young of *Musician* observed in a prescient article written during the band's tour of America in 1984:

It's hard to imagine two guys with less in common psychologically, yet together they seem to make a complete personality. Extrovert balanced by introvert, logic by intuition, entertainment balanced by artistry. Sometimes it comes together, which is thrilling, and sometimes it sounds like all four of them are playing different songs as fast as possible, which is pretty funny. Attempts at intricate ensemble playing – such as vocal/guitar duels – appear to leave the participants as bewildered as if they were actually talking to each other.[7]

Significantly, in terms of Roth's Zen-like pursuit of the childlike mind, not to mention the kind of receptivity to 'the moment' that this implied, the move to Eddie's studio can only have represented a loss of an innocence that had been maintained throughout previous years, when the band still rehearsed in the basement of Roth's father's house. That arrangement had maintained a connection to their origins, and perhaps aspirations, as teenagers in Pasadena in the early 1970s.

The sense of time and distance that had elapsed by 1984 was also evident in small details – some of them obscure and little known. One favourite is a promo video for Miloš Forman's film *Amadeus* (1984), which took the form of a compilation of pop music video clips of the time which had been set to the music of Mozart, and inter-cut with scenes from the movie – all in an attempt to try to take the film to the new MTV audience. Roth appears in a specially filmed segment at the beginning as an absurd conductor dressed in a ludicrous cheetah-patterned suit and bow tie; tumbling onstage like one of the Three Stooges, he brushes himself down and gathers his composure before rapping the conductor's baton against a music stand and saying 'all right gentlemen, I have to get this suit back by five, so let's get it right the first time.' This was exactly what he was no longer able to do with Van Halen.

In the summer of 1984 between the end of Van Halen's North American tour and the first of a handful of shows they were scheduled to play in Europe during August and September, Eddie and Landee were laying down the soundtrack for another film, titled *The Wild Life* and directed by Cameron Crowe. Not content to sit around and wait again, Roth went into the studio with Templeman to cut some songs for his own EP, *Crazy from the Heat*.

As if to emphasize the growing separation of Roth from the Van Halen camp, *Rolling Stone* magazine, in its 'Random Notes' column, reported on a birthday party he threw in Manhattan – three months before the actual date – where he celebrated with the likes of Edgar Winter (who had been working with him on his solo sessions), members of The B-52S and a little-known singer named Madonna who was at the time working on her first album with Roth's friend Nile Rodgers. At the end of December 1984, Warner Bros released Roth's four-track EP (featuring covers of tunes by Louis Prima, The Lovin' Spoonful, Edgar Winter and The Beach Boys), which sailed high on the Billboard album charts and went on to sell more than one million copies in the first few months of its release. Roth's version of 'California Girls', propelled by a video that he had storyboarded and directed himself on Venice Beach, also hit number two on the Hot 100, much to the consternation of Eddie, who had no idea that this little side-project might take off in such a way.

The singer used Van Halen's downtime to do interviews for *Crazy from the Heat* at Van Halen's Hollywood offices, which – as if to emphasize who the star of the show really was – was also home to a replica statue of Michelangelo's *David*, which journalists encountered on their arrival. One such visitor, Mick Brown of the *Sunday Times Magazine*, reported being treated to excerpts from a book Roth had to hand, *200 of the World's Greatest Speeches – a Compendium of Discourse from Caesar to Martin Luther King*, in between which the singer expounded on his philosophy of rock 'n'roll. In addition to all this activity, Brown reported, Roth had lined up a cameo role as a grouchy cook in an upcoming film version of the kids' TV show *Sesame Street* (which fell through as a result of events that would unfold in early 1985). It all seemed symptomatic of the fact that Roth was now openly in competition with Eddie.

On the strength of his solo success and the videos he had directed Roth had signed a contract with CBS pictures to direct a movie, also titled *Crazy from the Heat,* and was handed a not insignificant budget of $25 million. It was a project for which he envisioned Van Halen providing the songs – not merely the soundtrack – along the lines of how Prince had used music in *Purple Rain*; that is, as set pieces with the band playing in the film, too. The fact that Roth was now taken up with this idea of starring in and directing a film sat uneasily with the others – it just seemed to confirm that he was trying to reassert his position as the star of the band. As a result of this stand-off between Roth and the others, he walked out on Van Halen in April 1985 and for six months or so Eddie believed that the band was over for good. He was convinced – at first – that, without Roth, the band would sink. Warner Bros seemed to agree and even asked the band initially to consider not using the name 'Van Halen' if they decided to continue with another singer, so integral had Roth been to how the company perceived the band (not to mention how they felt the band to be seen in the eyes of the public). Roth's replacement would turn out to be Sammy Hagar, once of San Francisco-based band Montrose, protégés of Templeman and an early influence on Van Halen, who had been recording as a solo artist since leaving Montrose in the mid-1970s. Oddly enough, although he and Roth had never met in person they had, over the previous five years, sporadically traded insults via the pages of the music press in the UK.

Van Halen, without Roth, continued much as they had left off, releasing five multi-platinum albums in the US; four of them number ones – until the relationship between Eddie and singer Hagar began to decline during their tour in 1995, when Hagar would find himself arriving at sound check to be greeted by 'subtle' hints that maybe he was no longer welcome in the band – as the brothers Van Halen broke into old Roth-era tunes like 'Beautiful Girls' and 'Hot for Teacher' right at the moment he walked onstage. That relationship was severed in the midst of recriminations about recording schedules in June 1996.

The rear sleeve of *Montrose* (1973) by Montrose, produced by Ted Templeman and featuring his sometime Van Morrison session players, Ronnie Montrose and Bill Church – and, more significantly, David Lee Roth's replacement in 1985, Sammy Hagar.

For Roth, the demise of Van Halen was soon followed by the collapse of his film project, as CBS Pictures went bust. At the time he had been working with Nile Rodgers, the former leader of 1970s disco band, Chic, who was composing the soundtrack to the *Crazy from the Heat* film.[8] With the film now a distant possibility, his hand was forced, and he began to put together his own hard rock outfit, which released, in 1986, the first of a series of successful albums that gradually produced diminishing sales returns.

The whole point of Roth's approach to rock'n'roll, to being in a band, was to lose himself. Eddie had given him the freedom and opportunity to do this and, clearly, he did something of the same order for the guitarist. When they separated, they were forced into their own limitations, and compelled to work at creativity in a way that they never had known before. Shades of the old exuberance were there in some of Roth's solo records, but it seemed that whoever his new musical partners might be, they would be unable to create the conditions in which he could forget himself, and were incapable of providing him with musical parts that seemed made for his eclectic tastes, as had been the case with Van Halen, whose output, as Charles Young noted in 1984, was 'highly eccentric' by rock standards.[9] In those post-Roth years, the output of Van Halen also – despite continued success – sounded like the work of a band whose best days were over. Perhaps too much success had made them too comfortable, an effect not really felt during the Roth years because they were never allowed the time to stop and reflect on it all, to become really conscious of what they were doing.

Almost ten years after Roth split with Van Halen there were signs that Eddie was beginning to warm to the idea of working together again. In a *Rolling Stone* interview he was fairly complimentary about the singer, saying Roth was 'a very creative guy' whose contribution to the band had been undeniable. 'Working with him was not a problem', he told David Wild. 'It was living with the guy.'[10] This slight change of perspective may have had a lot to do with a chance meeting that took place between the two men on the streets of New York City in 1994. Eddie and his wife were walking along Madison Avenue early one morning when they passed a familiar-looking figure whose head was partially con-cealed by a hood. After a bit, they stopped in their tracks as Eddie suddenly realized that he had just passed Roth – here, of all places, thousands of miles from where they grew up together. But by 1994, Roth had returned to Greenwich Village, where he was living and recording an album titled *Your Filthy Little Mouth*, with Nile Rodgers as producer.

Eddie called back to the hooded figure a few times and, eventually, Roth responded, slowly walking back to greet his old partner. Both sides said it was an amiable meeting. Eddie asked about Roth's new record, which featured a mutual friend, a guitar player from their early days in Pasadena, Terry Kilgore (who had been in Roth's band of 1971–3, Red Ball Jets). 'He was kind of hesitant', Eddie said of Roth. 'I shook his hand. I asked him how he was doing and he looked kinda shocked. It's like a divorce. It's over and done with.' Eddie seemed content to have been able, in some way, to talk to him again without it degenerating into name-calling, and pointedly said that 'anyone who thinks he's ever going to come back is ridiculous'.[11]

Within little more than a year, however, Roth was back and the Van Halen brothers and Mike Anthony were working with him once again at Eddie's studio in the Hollywood hills, just off Coldwater Canyon. However, it would be a short-lived affair that didn't extend beyond their first appearance in public, when the two had a falling-out backstage at the MTV Awards ceremony in 1996 after Roth had been rather too enthusiastic in lapping up the standing ovation the band received when they appeared onstage to present an award to Beck Hansen. While clearly stung by this turn of events, and after exchanging insults in public once again, Roth still seemed to have conflicted feelings about his old bandmate.

Some months after the MTV fiasco, Roth was caught on TV at a New York film premiere with DJ Howard Stern and Tony Bennett, standing in front of the press with a large and boisterous crowd behind them. Grabbing a microphone, Stern shouted to the crowd, 'Van Halen is nothing without David Lee Roth'. Then, gesturing to the crowd, he started chanting, 'Eddie sucks, Eddie sucks, Eddie sucks', to the bemusement of Bennett and the discomfort of Roth as the crowd loudly and enthusiastically picked up the chant. He eventually grabbed the microphone and said: 'Wait a minute, hang on. Eddie doesn't suck. He just made a mistake.' Roth still didn't like anyone putting down 'his team', no matter how far apart they now seemed.

Four years later the two would meet again in an effort to find a way of working together. During their discussions, when Eddie was also undergoing treatment for tongue cancer, it was reported that they had been spotted having meetings at a Sunset Strip night

Eddie Van Halen and David Lee Roth, by then in their mid-50s, pictured onstage again for the first time in 24 years, 2008. An unseen Alex Van Halen was still behind the drums, but bass player Michael Anthony was replaced by Eddie's sixteen-year-old son, Wolfgang.

club.[12] During this time – around the year 2000 – the band, along with Roth, worked again on new songs in the 5150 studio, reportedly recording an album's worth of material with The Dust Brothers (producers of Beck's *Odelay* album) – but it ended again in acrimony without the results ever being made public. Lawyers had been engaged by Roth after it was discovered that a deal had been cut with Warner Bros in the mid-1990s over Van Halen's Roth-era catalogue, which saw the rest of the band reaping comparative riches for continuing sales as Roth earned a mere 30 cents per album sold.

After those two aborted reunion attempts, during which Roth would return to that little studio up on Coldwater Canyon Avenue and ultimately leave again frustrated, he would mockingly refer to it as 'the siege of Howdy-Doody Mountain' (after the TV puppet show *Howdy Doody* from the 1950s) his not-so-subtle side-swipe at Van Halen's need for some direction, for the return of the original puppet-master. In 1997 he suggested that the attempted reunion foundered because Eddie was neither ready to take on the mantle of boss, nor willing to let Roth do so. 'What's happening up there on Howdy-Doody Mountain is that there's an ego problem – they don't have one.'[13]

In September 2006 Eddie made a bizarre appearance on Howard Stern's SIRIUS radio show, during which he claimed to have found a cure for the tongue cancer that he had been battling in recent years. It was the result, he said, of work conducted at a research lab he had supposedly established in Long Island, New York. When pressed on exactly what this cure was and why it hadn't been communicated to the medical profession at large, Eddie replied gnomically, 'I'd tell you, but they'd throw me in jail. It ain't legal.' When Stern asked Eddie if he was ever going to work again with Roth – 'Diamond Dave', Stern said, using the singer's nickname – he laughed and shot back, 'you mean *Cubic Zirconia?*'

It was a reference to a fake diamond that sailed over Stern's head, revealing perhaps that Eddie was not as befuddled as impressions suggested. 'I'm open to anything', he said. 'The guy's like a loose cannon – but, hey, I can deal with loose cannons.'

After 30-odd minutes of this, Eddie disappeared, as Stern and his gang discussed the intractable weirdness of the relationships surrounding Van Halen and its various former band members. Someone then piped up: 'Imagine being around David Lee Roth all fuckin' day and night. That must be insanity.' Stern, who knew Roth quite well, and wasn't exactly shy and retiring himself, agreed: 'I'd bang my head into a wall . . . 'cos he's David Lee Roth 24 hours a day.' By this time in 2006, however, Roth was living out a life that seemed far removed from his 'Diamond Dave' persona, and – like Eddie – dabbling in his own small way with the medical profession. The singer, it seemed, would occasionally trade his microphone for an ambulance, as he rode the streets of New York as a fully trained-up and qualified volunteer Emergency Medical Technician, coming to the rescue of what one can only imagine must have been baffled sick people.

These episodes, though, were only preludes to the inevitable reconciliation that was bound to succeed one time, at least. During early 2007 Van Halen with Roth began rehearsing for a tour that would begin in September of that year. Later, after the tour was underway, they were nominated for induction to the Rock and Roll Hall of Fame – that institution set up in the late 1980s to confer some kind of ultimate approval on a small handful of performers each year who had been adjudged to have stood the test of time (a performer could only be nominated 25 years after their first recordings). Along with REM, Patti Smith and Grandmaster Flash, they were to be officially inducted at a ceremony in March 2008. These televised events had, in previous years, been occasions where old friends and enemies were reunited to perform for an audience made up of fellow artists and other music business luminaries. However, for Van Halen, predictably, it never quite panned out according to the norm.

None of the then current members of the band – Roth and Eddie and Alex Van Halen – bothered to show up to collect their gong and reap the applause. Only Mike Anthony and Sammy Hagar, recently slammed by Eddie for touring together and playing Van Halen songs as 'The Other Half', turned up. 'The other half of Van Halen is my brother', an exasperated Eddie told Howard Stern. 'They're out there playing my tunes and selling tequila and hot sauce.' That was a reference to the commercial interests of his two former bandmates who were, indeed, producing their own alcohol and barbecue condiments. Hagar's Tequila, named after a Van Halen song called 'Cabo Wabo' (and his resort club in Cabo San Lucas, Baja California), had started as a small hand-made operation, but generated huge riches for the singer as it garnered a host of awards for excellence. It was so successful that he sold a majority share of it for $80 million in 2008.

As for Van Halen's non-appearance at the Rock and Roll Hall of Fame – in retrospect it all seemed to fit with the aesthetics of this Zen-like attitude of 'non-graspingness', which went along just fine with the 'do not care' ethos of rock'n'roll. No matter if some of them really did want to be there, it seemed in keeping with the spirit of the original Van Halen members *not* to show up. In the twenty-odd years of its existence the only other inductees to snub the Rock and Roll Hall of Fame ceremony were the Sex Pistols, the year previously. But as Roth had said at the Us Festival press conference all those years before, in 1983 – in between barbs aimed at The Clash – 'We never cared what anybody thought about anything. We'll sail down our merry little path and you're all invited, but I'm driving.'[14]

CHRONOLOGY

1950s

Alex Van Halen born, Amsterdam, Holland (May, 1953)
Michael Anthony born, Chicago, Illinois (June, 1954)
David Lee Roth born, Bloomington, Indiana (October, 1954)
Edward Van Halen born, Amsterdam, Holland (January, 1955)

1960s

The Van Halens emigrate from Holland to Pasadena, California (1962)
David Lee Roth and Michael Anthony, with their families, move to Pasadena
and Arcadia, California (early 1960s)

1973

David Lee Roth joins Eddie and Alex Van Halen in a band then named Mammoth.
He persuades the brothers to rename the band Van Halen.

1974

Michael Anthony joins as bass player. The band begin a long-standing residency
at Gazzarri's on the Sunset Strip (April), playing multiple sets a night several
times a week for two and a half years.

1976

Demo recordings are made at Electric Ladyland, New York and the Village
Recorder, Los Angeles, produced by Gene Simmons with a view to Van Halen
signing with Casablanca Records. It comes to nothing.

In December Van Halen become one of the first bands to play the recently re-opened
Whisky A Go Go on Sunset Strip. They play 30-plus shows at the venue in the next
year, and make a final appearance in early 1978 before the release of *Van Halen*.

1977

The band is signed to Warner Brothers Records by staff producer Ted Templeman and company president Mo Ostin.

Van Halen is recorded at Sunset Sound Recorders, Hollywood, late in the year (and released March 1978). The album goes on to achieve 'diamond' status for 10-million-plus sales in the USA.

1978

The band embarks on their first world tour, playing outside California for the first time.

Van Halen II recorded at Sunset Sound Recorders in December and released the following February.

1979

Women and Children First recorded at Sunset Sound in December and released the following March.

1980

Roth begins frequenting the Zero-Zero club, an after-hours club that masquerades as an art gallery during the daytime. He becomes the club's 'anonymous financial benefactor'.

1981

Fair Warning recorded at Sunset Sound (February) and released (April).

1982

Diver Down recorded at the turn of the year at Hollywood Recorders, and released in April.

1983

Eddie Van Halen and Donn Landee convert a racquetball court at Eddie's home in the Hollywood Hills into the studio where the next Van Halen album will to be recorded.

Van Halen play the Us Festival, 31 May. *The Guinness Book of World Records* later lists the appearance as the highest paid concert performance in history (the band were paid a then record fee of $1.5m).

Sessions for MCMLXXXIV/1984, Van Halen's sixth album, are drawn out over the period April–September. The album is released on the last weekend of the year.

1984

MCMLXXXIV/1984 becomes Van Halen's most successful album, selling eight million copies worldwide in its first ten months of release.

David Lee Roth records *Crazy from the Heat,* a 4-song EP, in New York (August).

1985

Roth scores top 5 hits on both the singles and the albums charts (January-April), and is handed a $25million budget by CBS Pictures to write, direct and star in a film with the working title *Crazy From the Heat.* The film never makes it past pre-production as CBS Pictures goes bankrupt.

David Lee Roth leaves Van Halen in April. He is eventually replaced by singer Sammy Hagar, who goes on to front a rather different Van Halen for the next 11 years.

1996

David Lee Roth records two new songs with Van Halen for a compilation album.

An apparently reunited Van Halen makes a first public appearance, at an MTV Awards ceremony in New York. Appearing onstage to hand out an award, they receive a standing ovation, but soon after they fall apart again after a disagreement backstage between Roth and Eddie Van Halen.

2000

David Lee Roth records with Van Halen again at Eddie's Coldwater Canyon studio. Although a reunion is never announced, and knowledge of the sessions only leaks out after the fact, it is later rumoured that they recorded an album's worth of new material. The band splits again, and the results never see the light of day.

2006

It is announced publicly that Roth has re-joined Van Halen in preparation for a tour that travels across the USA during 2007 and 2008.

Michael Anthony discovers – on the Internet – that he has been replaced as bass player by Eddie's 15-year-old son, Wolfgang.

2007

Van Halen are inducted into the Rock and Roll Hall of Fame, but none of the current members of the band show up to collect their award. Former Van Halen members Michael Anthony and Sammy Hagar, however, do appear at the ceremony.

2010

The reclusive David Lee Roth is photographed at the Scottish Highland Games in Pleasanton, California, where – bizarrely – it turns out that he is competing in the sheepdog trials ('the precise herding of sheep by highly trained dogs and their handlers').

2011

Without any official public announcement, it is revealed that Van Halen began recording a new album with Roth in January.

2012

Van Halen's seventh album with David Lee Roth, *A Different Kind of Truth* – their first in nearly three decades – is released early in February to overwhelmingly enthusiastic reviews, many of which express astonishment at how ageless the band sound. *The Guardian* judged the album a 'frequently thrilling' return, whose songs 'crackle, fizz and bulge with priapic exuberance, and not just due to the reliably demented Roth. Seemingly inspired by the presence of his 20-year-old son Wolfgang on bass, [Eddie] Van Halen is on extraordinary form.'

REFERENCES

PREFACE

1 Peter Goddard, the rock and jazz critic for the *Toronto Star*, in Philip Kamin and Peter Goddard, *Van Halen* (London, 1984), p. 104.
2 Mike Nicholls, 'Gypsy Lee Roth', *Record Mirror* (7 July 1979).
3 Kevin Starr, *Coast of Dreams: A History of Contemporary California* (London, 2005), pp. 10–26.

1 OUT UPON THE OCEAN

1 Geoff Barton, 'New Boots and (Stretch) Panties', *Sounds* (28 June 1980), p. 18.
2 Charles M. Young, 'The Oddest Couple: Can It Last', *Musician* (July 1984), p. 47.
3 Lewis Hyde, *Trickster Makes This World* (New York, 1988), pp. 7–8.
4 Quoted in William J. Hynes and William G. Doty, eds, *Mythical Trickster Figures: Contours, Contexts and Criticisms* (Tuscaloosa, AL, 1993), p. 1.
5 Scott Cohen, 'It's Only Roth'n'Roll', *Spin* (April 1996), p. 75.
6 Hyde, *Trickster Makes This World*, pp. 6–7.
7 Young, 'The Oddest Couple', p. 52.
8 Don Waller, '*Diver Down* is Up with the Best', *Los Angeles Times* (2 May 1982), p. k66.
9 Henry Rollins, *Do I Come Here Often?* (Los Angeles, CA, 1998), p. 28.
10 Ibid.
11 Steven Daly, 'Mr Saturday Night', *GQ Magazine* (October 1996), p. 156.
12 Timothy White, 'Van Halen's Thud Rock', *Rolling Stone*, 295 (12 July 1979).
13 Cynthia Rose, 'Van Halen: *Diver Down*', *New Musical Express* (8 May 1982). Emphasis mine.
14 Cynthia Rose, 'Van Halen: *Fair Warning*', *New Musical Express* (20 June 1981).
15 Ibid.

16 Don Waller, 'Van Halen: Life with the Top Down', *Los Angeles Times* (5 February 1984), p. k64.

17 Cynthia Rose, 'Van Halen: MCMLXXXIV', *New Musical Express* (March 1984).

18 Ibid.

19 Barney Hoskyns, 'I Was a Teenage Gristleburger!', *New Musical Express* (25 August 1984).

20 Dave DiMartino, 'Remnants of the Flesh Hangover: If You Hate Van Halen, You're Wrong', *Creem* (July 1980).

21 Hyde, *Trickster Makes This World*, pp. 6–7.

22 A. C. Rhodes, 'The Bink Generation: Dave DiMartino in Conversation, Pt IV', (2008), at http://rockcritics.com (last accessed April 2009).

23 Steve Rosen, *Rock Talk, Vol. 1, Issue 1: Eddie Van Halen and David Lee Roth*, 1980 (digital audio music magazine) (Stoneworks, CA, 2007)

24 Barton, 'New Boots and (Stretch) Panties', p. 17.

25 Kevin Starr, *Coast of Dreams: A History of Contemporary California* (London, 2005), p. 11–13.

26 Daisetz Teitaro Suzuki, 'Foreword', in Eugen Herrigel, *Zen in the Art of Archery*, trans. R.F.C. Hull (London, 1975), p. 7.

2 ISLANDS: SUNSET STRIP AND THE 1970S, C. 1974–7

1 Barney Hoskyns, 'Boulevard of Broken Dreams: A Trip Down Sunset Strip', *Mojo* (January 1994).

2 Domenic Priore, *Riot on Sunset Strip* (London, 2007), p. 18.

3 Drew Tewksbury, 'Reverberations and Echo Chambers', *Flaunt Magazine*, 84 (2007).

4 Eric Avila, *Popular Culture in the Age of White Flight: Fear and Fantasy in Suburban Los Angeles* (Berkeley, CA, 2004), p. 226.

5 Mike Davis, 'Riot Nights on Sunset Strip', *The Reader Extra* (December 2008)

6 Priore, *Riot on Sunset Strip*, p. 242.

7 See Michael Walker, *Laurel Canyon: The Inside Story of Rock-and-Roll's Legendary Neighborhood* (London, 2007).

8 See Priore, *Riot on Sunset Strip*.

9 Ibid., p. 257.

10 See Edward D. Berkowitz, *Something Happened: A Political and Cultural Overview of the Seventies* (New York, 2007)

11 Sam Binkley, *Getting Loose: Lifestyle Consumption in the 1970s* (Durham, NC, 2007), p. 5.

12 See Barney Hoskyns, *Hotel California: The Story of the Los Angeles Music Scene* (London, 1996).

13 Walker, *Laurel Canyon*, p. 166.

14 Ibid., p. 183.

15 Eddie Van Halen recalled the event in an interview with Jas Obrecht. See *Van Halen: Best of Guitar Player* (San Francisco, CA, 1993), p. 19.

16 Danny Sugerman, *Wonderland Avenue: Tales of Glamour and Excess* (London, 1989), p. 240.

17 See Phast Phreddie Patterson, 'Phast Freddie's Hollywood (Circa 1973–1983)', at rocksbackpages.com (originally written in 1996 but unpublished, last accessed April 2009).

18 Barney Hoskyns, *Waiting for the Sun: The Story of the Los Angeles Music Scene* (London, 1996), pp. 70–71.

19 See Jerry Bloom, *Black Knight: Ritchie Blackmore* (London, 2008), pp. 172–4.

20 Hoskyns, *Waiting for the Sun*, p. 251.

21 Sugerman, *Wonderland Avenue*, p. 241.

22 Kim Fowley, 'King of the Nighttime World', at rocksbackpages.com (last accessed April 2009).

23 Ibid.

24 See Lisa L. Rhodes, *Electric Ladyland: Women and Rock Culture* (Philadelphia, PA, 2005), pp. 225–30.

25 Sugerman, *Wonderland Avenue*, p. 241.

26 Recalled by Kid Congo Powers (of Los Angeles band, The Gun Club), in Hoskyns, 'Boulevard of Broken Dreams', at rocksbackpages.com (last accessed April 2009).

27 See Legs McNeil and Gillian McCain, *Please Kill Me: The Uncensored Oral History of Punk* (London, 1997), p. 310.

28 Fowley, 'King of the Nighttime World'.

29 Ibid.

30 See Terry Atkinson, 'Breaking out of Bar-band gigs', *Los Angeles Times* (27 December 1977), p. g8.

31 Patterson, 'Van Halen's Back Door Rock'n'Roll'.

32 Gibson Keddie, 'Stand By Your Man: Mike Anthony', *Guitarist* (May 1993), p. 114.

33 Sylvie Simmons, 'Halen High Water', *Sounds* (26 June 1982).

34 Hoskyns, *Waiting for the Sun*, p. 325.

35 Steven Blush, 'David Lee Roth', *Seconds*, 26 (1994), p. 35.

36 When Van Halen reformed with Roth in 2007 for a tour of the USA they chose as their opening act Ky-Mani Marley, one of Bob Marley's sons.

37 Hoskyns, *Waiting for the Sun*, p. 296.

38 Ibid., p. 285.

39 Walker, *Laurel Canyon*, pp. 60–61.

40 Richard Cromelin, 'L.A. Rock Resurgence', *Los Angeles Times* (18 December 1976), p. b10.

41 Harvey Kubernik, *Hollywood Shack Job* (Albuquerque, NM, 2006), pp. 75–6.

42 Rodney Bingenheimer, *Phonograph Record* (December 1976), p. 8.

43 Cromelin, 'L.A. Rock Resurgence', p. b10.

44 Steven Rosen, 'Van Halen', *Record Review* (April 1979), p. 8.

45 Hoskyns, *Waiting for the Sun*, p. 285.

46 Richard Cromelin, 'Van Halen Keeps Asserting Itself', *Los Angeles Times* (29 January 1977), p. b7.

47 Christopher Hurley, 'Wanna Borrow My Guitar?', *The Inside*, 16 (Summer 2000).

3 THE GOLDEN DREAM, CALIFORNIA

1 Dana Polan, 'California through the Lens of Hollywood', in *Reading California: Art, Image and Identity, 1900–2000*, ed. Stephanie Barron, Sheri Bernstein and Ilene Susan Fort (Berkeley, CA, 2000), p. 129.

2 Blake Allmendinger, 'All About Eden', in *Reading California*, p. 113.

3 See, for example, Norman M. Klein, *The History of Forgetting: Los Angeles and the Erasure of Memory* (London, 1997), chapter One.

4 Douglas Cazaux Sackman, *Orange Empire: California and the Fruits of Eden* (Berkeley, CA, 2003), p. 23.

5 Kevin Starr, *Inventing the Dream: California through the Progressive Era* (Oxford, 1985), p. 99.

6 Carey McWilliams, *Southern California: An Island of the Land* (Salt Lake City, UT), p. 108.

7 See Erik Davis, *The Visionary State: A Journey Through California's Spiritual Landscape,* with photographs by Michael Rauner (San Francisco, CA, 2006).

8 Quoted in McWilliams, *Southern California*, p. 249.

9 Quoted in Davis, *The Visionary State*, p. 77.

10 In Kevin Starr, 'Carey McWilliams's California: The Light and the Dark', in *Reading California*, p. 18.

11 On 'spiritual' California, see Davis, *The Visionary State*.

12 See Carey McWilliams, *California: The Great Exception* (Berkeley, CA, 1999), p. 61.

13 Charles Jencks, *Heteropolis* (London, 1993), p. 24.

14 Mike Davis, quotation from the jacket of McWilliams, *California: The Great Exception*. Emphasis mine.

15 Starr, *Inventing the Dream*, p. 99.

16 McWilliams, *Southern California*, p. 101.

17 Quoted in Philip Kamin and Peter Goddard, *Van Halen* (London, 1984), p. 15.

18 Allmendinger, 'All About Eden', p. 113.

19 For instance, in Steve Rosen, 'Van Halen', *Record Review* (April 1979).

20 See the interview in Kamin and Goddard, *Van Halen*, pp. 98–121.

21 David Wild, 'Balancing Act: Eddie Van Halen, the Rolling Stone Interview', *Rolling Stone*, 705 (April 1995), p. 46.

22 See Marlene De Vries, 'Why Ethnicity? The Ethnicity of Dutch Eurasians Raised in the Netherlands', in *Culture, Structure and Beyond: Changing Identities and Social Positions of Immigrants and Their Children*, ed. Maurice Crul, Flip Lindo and Chin Lin Pang (Amsterdam, 1999), p. 37–9.

23 Ibid.

24 See Mark Taylor Brinsfield, 'A Dutch Eurasian Revival?', in *The Sum of Our Parts: Mixed-Heritage Asian-Americans*, ed. Teresa Williams-Leon and Cynthia L. Nakashima (Philadelphia, PA, 2001), p. 197.

25 Brinsfield, 'A Dutch Eurasian Revival?', p. 197.

26 De Vries, 'Why Ethnicity?', pp. 37–8.

27 Brinsfield, 'A Dutch Eurasian Revival?', p. 205.

28 Wild, 'Balancing Act', p. 46.

29 The Derek and the Dominoes bootleg is *Stormy Monday: Civic Auditorium, Santa Monica, CA, November 20, 1970*, on Paddington Records 040/041/042.

30 Martin Booe, 'Rock'n'Roll in Their Hearts', *Los Angeles Times* (23 November 2003).

31 Roth, *Crazy from the Heat*, p. 61.

32 Ibid., p. 60.

33 Debby Miller, 'Van Halen's Split Personality', *Rolling Stone*, 424 (June 1984), p. 77.

34 Fred 'Phast Phreddie' Patterson, 'Van Halen's Back Door Rock'n'Roll', *Wax Paper* (1978), at rocksbackpages.com (accessed April 2009)

35 Booe, 'Rock'n'Roll in Their Hearts'.

4 HANGING TEN, C. 1977–82

1 Hildegarde Flanner, 'Noon on Alameda Street', in *Many Californias: Literature from the Golden State*, ed. Gerald W. Haslam (Reno, NV, 1992), pp. 91–2.

2 Ibid.

3 Neil Zlozower, *Van Halen: A Visual History* (San Francisco, CA, 2008), p. 33.

4 David Gans, 'Ted Templeman', *BAM* (9 October 1981), n.p.

5   W. T. Lhamon Jr, *Deliberate Speed: The Origin of a Cultural Style in the American 1950s* (Washington, DC, and London, 1990), p. 31.

6   Dave Simons, 'Tales from the Top: Van Halen's *Van Halen*', *Songwriter 101*: at http://songwriter101.com (last accessed April 2009).

7   Tim Hollis and Greg Ehrbar, *Mouse Tracks: The Story of Walt Disney Records* (Jackson, MS, 2006), p. 58.

8   Simons, 'Tales from the Top'.

9   '100 Greatest Guitar Songs of All Time', *Rolling Stone*, 1054 (12 June 2008).

10 Robert Walser, *Running with the Devil: Power, Gender and Madness in Heavy Metal Music* (Middletown, CT, 1993), pp. 69–70.

11 Peter Manning, *Electronic and Computer Music* (Oxford, 2004), p. 170.

12 Quoted in William Clark and Jim Cogan, *Temples of Sound: Inside the Great Recording Studios* (San Francisco, CA, 2003), p. 49.

13 Ibid., p. 48.

14 James Riordan and Jerry Prochnicky, *Break On Through: The Life and Death of Jim Morrison* (London, 1991), p. 111.

15 Gans, 'Ted Templeman'.

16 See Donn Landee's account in Simons, 'Tales from the Top'.

17 Simons, 'Tales from the Top'.

18 Gans, 'Ted Templeman'.

19 'Recording Costs Rising', *Los Angeles Times* (22 October 1978).

20 See Barney Hoskyns, *Waiting for the Sun: The Story of the Los Angeles Music Scene* (London, 1996), pp. 199–205.

21 R. Serge Denisoff, *Tarnished Gold: The Record Industry Revisited* (Edison, NK, 1986), p. 167.

22 Denisoff, *Tarnished Gold*, p. 158.

23 Gene Sculatti, 'Harpers Bizarre: Feelin' Groovy' (sleevenotes) (Warner Bros Records, 1997).

24 Joseph Lanza, *Vanilla Pop: Sweet Sounds from Frankie Avalon to ABBA* (Chicago, IL, 2005), p. 143.

25 See Hoskyns, *Waiting for the Sun*, pp. 199–205.

26 Victor Bockris and John Cale, *What's Welsh for Zen: The Autobiography of John Cale* (London, 2000), p. 138.

27 Gans, 'Ted Templeman'.

28 Jeff Kitts, Brad Tolinski and Harold Steinblatt, eds, *Guitar World Presents Van Halen* (Milwaukee, WI, 1997) p. 14.

29 Steve Rosen, *Rock Talk, Vol. 1, Issue 1: Eddie Van Halen and David Lee Roth, 1980* (digital audio music magazine) (Stoneworks, CA, 2007).

30 Ibid.

31 Timothy White, 'Van Halen's Thud Rock', *Rolling Stone*, 295 (12 July 1979).

32 Ibid.

33 Bud Scoppa, 'The Little Feat Saga', an essay accompanying Rhino Records' Little Feat retrospective *Hotcakes and Outtakes: 30 Years of Little Feat* (2000).

34 Ibid.

35 Dave Queen, 'Van Halen: Diver Down', *Stylus* (2005): at www.stylusmagazine.com (last accessed April 2009).

5 HOLLYWOOD FLOTSAM, *C.* 1980–82

1 Don Waller, 'In Search of the Elephant's Balls', in *Make the Music Go Bang! The Early LA Punk Scene*, ed. Don Snowden, with photographs by Gary Leonard (New York, 1997), p. 123.

2 Mick Farren, 'LA Punk', *New Musical Express* (11 April 1981).

3 Ibid.

4 Brendan Mullen, 'Nightmare in Punk Alley', in *Make the Music Go Bang!*, p. 82.

5 Ibid., p. 82.

6 Ibid., p. 83.

7 Waller, 'In Search of the Elephant's Balls', p. 155.

8 Marc Spitz and Brendan Mullen, *We Got the Neutron Bomb: The Untold Story of LA Punk* (New York, 2001), p. 243.

9 Dave Queen, 'Van Halen: Diver Down', *Stylus* (2005): at www.stylusmagazine.com (last accessed April 2009), and Geoff Barton, New Boots and (Stretch) Panties', *Sounds* (28 June 1980), p. 18.

10 Lina Lecaro, 'Lights and Flash', *LA Weekly* (24 January 2008).

11 Mullen, 'Nightmare in Punk Alley', p. 84.

12 Pleasant Gehman, 'Party at Ground Zero Zero', in *Make the Music Go Bang!*, p. 136.

13 Spitz and Mullen, *We Got the Neutron Bomb*, p. 255.

14 Ibid.

15 Ibid.

16 Mullen, 'Nightmare in Punk Alley', p. 84.

17 Don Waller, 'Top Jimmy is for Real', *Los Angeles Times* (5 February 1984), p. k63.

18 Art Fein, *The LA Musical History Tour: A Guide to the Rock and Roll Landmarks of Los Angeles* (San Francisco, CA, 2001), p. 28.

19 Don Snowden, 'Blues Rooting: Top Jimmy and the Rhythm Pigs', *Boston Phoenix* (16 October 1987).

20 Danny Weizmann, 'Pig Music for Beer People: Top Jimmy', *Flipside* (1981).
21 Joe Keithley, *I Shithead: A Life in Punk* (Vancouver, BC, 2003), p. 93.
22 Fred 'Phast Phreddie' Patterson, 'Like Everything Else in Los Angeles, It is Now a Mini Mall', in *Make the Music Go Bang!*, p. 28.
23 The photographs illustrate the book *Make the Music Go Bang!*
24 Waller, 'Top Jimmy is for Real', p. k63.
25 Ibid., p. k63.
26 Spitz and Mullen, *We Got the Neutron Bomb*, pp. 243–5.
27 Waller, 'In Search of the Elephant's Balls', p. 127.
28 Frank Meyer, 'Art and Struggle . . . But Mainly Nutso Debauch with David Lee Roth', *LA Weekly* (28 August 2003).
29 Mötley Crüe, *The Dirt: Confessions of the World's Most Notorious Rock Band* (New York, 2002), p. 4.

6 THE TAO OF DAVE: SURF LIFE

1 David Lee Roth, *Crazy from the Heat* (New York, 1997), p. 16.
2 Bob Spitz, *Dylan: A Biography* (New York, 1989), p. 122.
3 Nancy Collins, 'David Lee Roth: The Rolling Stone Interview', *Rolling Stone*, 445 (11 April 1985).
4 Dave Van Ronk with Elijah Wald, *The Mayor of MacDougal Street: A Memoir*, (Cambridge, MA, 2005), p. 158.
5 Bob Dylan, quoted in Clinton Heylin, *Bob Dylan: Behind the Shades Revisited* (New York, 2001), p. 54.
6 Bob Dylan, *Chronicles, Volume One* (London, 2004), pp. 10–11.
7 See Daniel Brockman, 'Voice of Regeneration: Richie Havens Rages On 40 Years After Woodstock', *The Boston Phoenix* (18 December 2008). See also, Spitz, *Dylan*, pp. 122–3.
8 Richie Havens, quoted in Keith Shadwick, *Jimi Hendrix* (San Francisco, MA, 2003), p. 23. In 1966, Havens sent Jimi Hendrix to Manny Roth at the Wha?, where the guitarist would eventually lead the venue's first house band for a short period before he went to London to make his name.
9 Brockman, 'Voice of Regeneration'.
10 Ibid.
11 Roth, *Crazy from the Heat*, p. 23.
12 Ibid., p. 39.
13 Ibid., p. 39.
14 Mike Wallace, 'Mike Wallace Asks Jack Kerouac: What is the Beat Genera-

tion?', in *Conversations with Jack Kerouac*, ed. Kevin J. Hughes (Jackson, MS, 2005), p. 3.

15 John Tytell, *Naked Angels: Kerouac, Ginsberg, Burroughs* (New York, 1976), p. 16.

16 Ibid., p. 16.

17 In Ann Charters, 'Introduction', in *The Portable Beat Reader* (New York, 1992), p. xxi.

18 W. T. Lhamon Jr, *Deliberate Speed: The Origins of a Cultural Style in the American 1950s* (New York, 1990), p. 10.

19 Don Waller, 'Van Halen: Life with the Top Down', *Los Angeles Times* (5 February 1984), p. k64.

20 Richard Meltzer, *The Aesthetics of Rock* [1970] (New York, 1987), p. 120.

21 Kerouac, from *On the Road*, quoted in Lhamon, *Deliberate Speed*, p. 165.

22 Robert Pattison, *The Triumph of Vulgarity: Rock Music in the Mirror of Romanticism* (Oxford and New York, 1987), pp. 117–18. Like Meltzer, Pattison sees such 'vulgarity' as a positive force.

23 Alan Watts, *The Way of Zen* (London, 1962), p. 47.

24 Terry Atkinson, 'Van Halen's Big Rock', *Rolling Stone*, 293 (14 June 1979), p. 14. Emphasis mine.

25 Watts, *The Way of Zen*, p. 41.

26 Daisetz T. Suzuki, *The Zen Doctrine of No-Mind* (York Beach, ME, 1972), p. 53.

27 In Kristine McKenna, 'Van Halen's David Lee Roth', *WET*, 34 (November–December 1981), p. 57.

28 Don Waller, 'Van Halen: Life with the Top Down', *Los Angeles Times* (5 February 1984), p. k62.

29 Reyner Banham, *Los Angeles: The Architecture of Four Ecologies* (London, 1971), p. 129.

30 Sanford Kwinter, *Architectures of Time: Towards a Theory of the Event in Modernist Culture* (Cambridge, MA, 2002), p. 28.

31 Mick Brown, 'The Secret of Van Halen's Excess', *Sunday Times Magazine* (20 January 1985).

32 Watts, *The Way of Zen*, p. 10.

33 Blush, 'David Lee Roth', p. 38. As Pattison noted: 'Vulgarity by its nature is impervious to condemnation.' *The Triumph of Vulgarity*, p. 3.

34 Steve Rosen, *Rock Talk, Vol. 1, Issue 1: Eddie Van Halen and David Lee Roth*, 1980 (digital audio music magazine) (Stoneworks, CA, 2007).

35 Ibid.

36 Geoff Barton, 'New Boots and (stretch) Panties', *Sounds* (28 June 1980), p. 17.

37 Philip Kamin and Peter Goddard, *Van Halen* (London, 1984), p. 109.

38 Tytell, *Naked Angels*, p. 22.

39 Kamin and Goddard, *Van Halen*, p. 100.

40 Ibid., p. 100.

41 Mikal Gilmore, 'Van Halen: the Endless Party', p. 204.

42 Debby Miller, 'Van Halen's Split Personality', *Rolling Stone*, 424 (21 June 1984),
    pp. 77–8.

43 Deborah Frost, 'David Lee Roth: Rock'n'Roll as a Contact Sport', *Record*
    (April 1984), p. 28.

44 Watts, *The Way of Zen*, pp. 41, 35.

45 Gerald Nicosia, *Memory Babe: A Critical Biography of Jack Kerouac* (Berkeley, CA,
    1997), p. 570.

7 DIVER DOWN, TEMPERATURE UP, *C*. 1981–2

1 Alan Watts, *The Way of Zen* (London, 1962), p. 10.

2 In the BBC film, 'Reyner Banham Loves Los Angeles' (1972). The film is archived
   online at: www.ubu.com.

3 Dave Queen, 'Van Halen: Diver Down', *Stylus* (2005): at
   www.stylusmagazine.com (last accessed April 2009).

4 Timothy White, *The Nearest Faraway Place: Brian Wilson, The Beach Boys and the
   Southern California Experience* (London, 1966), p. 271.

5 David Gans, 'What it Be, David Lee?', *Record* (April 1985), p. 26.

6 Ben Fong-Torres, 'David Lee Roth: Hyperactive, Irrepressible, Self-Satisfied',
   San Francisco Chronicle (10 February 1985).

7 Deborah Frost, 'David Lee Roth: Rock'n'Roll as a Contact Sport', *Record*
   (April 1984), p. 27.

8 Fong-Torres, 'David Lee Roth'.

9 David Wild, 'Balancing Act: Eddie Van Halen, The Rolling Stone Interview',
   Rolling Stone, 705 (April 1995), p. 46.

10 See Jeff Kitts, Brad Tolinski and Harold Steinblatt, eds, *Guitar World Presents
   Van Halen* (Milwaukee, WI, 1997), p. 20.

11 Dave DiMartino, 'Remnants of the Flesh Hangover: If You Hate Van Halen,
   You're Wrong', *Creem* (July 1980).

12 Davis Lee Roth, *Crazy from the Heat* (New York, 1997), p. 69.

13 Charles M. Young, 'Van Halen' review, *Rolling Stone* (4 May 1978).

14 Carey McWilliams, *California: The Great Exception* (Berkeley, CA, 1999), p. 4.

15 David Fricke, 'Can This Be Love?', *Rolling Stone*, 477 (3 July 1986), p. 33.

16 Steven Blush, 'David Lee Roth', *Seconds*, 26 (1994), p. 36.

17 Jordan McLachlan, 'King Edward', *Guitar* (March 1995), p. 126.

18 Steve Rosen, *Rock Talk, Vol. 1, Issue 1: Eddie Van Halen and David Lee Roth*, 1980 (digital audio music magazine) (Stoneworks, CA, 2007).

19 Ibid.

20 Barney Hoskyns, *Waiting for the Sun: The Story of the Los Angeles Music Scene* (London, 1996), p. 205ff.

21 Tom Beaujour, 'The Greatest Songs Ever: Hot For Teacher', *Blender* (November 2006).

22 H. P. Newquist, 'Edward Van Halen: The *Guitar* Interview', *Guitar* (March 1995), p. 121.

8 THINK LIKE THE WAVES, LIKE A CHILD, *C.* 1982–3

1 Dweezil Zappa, 'Sorcerer's Apprentice', *Guitar Player* (March 1995), p. 119.

2 David Gans, 'What it Be, David Lee?', *Record* (April 1985), p. 30.

3 Deborah Frost, 'David Lee Roth: Rock'n'Roll as a Contact Sport', *Record* (April 1984), p. 25.

4 Frost, 'David Lee Roth', p. 27.

5 Laura Canyon, 'Metal Daze', *Kerrang!*, 46 (14–27 July 1983), p. 22.

6 See Steve Wozniak with Gina Smith, *iWoz: How I Invented the Personal Computer, Co-founded Apple, and Had Fun Doing It* (New York, 2004), pp. 244–58.

7 Wesley G. Hughes and Richard West, 'Crowd Grows as Us Festival Turns to Heavy Metal', *Los Angeles Times* (30 May 1983).

8 Steve Rosen, 'Eddie Van Halen drops the bomb on Heavy Metal', *Guitar World* (January 1984).

9 Us Festival press conference, 31 May 1983.

10 Ibid.

11 Canyon, 'Metal Daze', p. 31.

12 John Mendelssohn, 'Us Festival '83: No More in '84', *Record* (Summer 1983), p. 8.

13 Vare, 'Clash, Van Halen Feud'.

14 Marcus Gray, *The Clash: Return of the Last Gang in Town* (London, 2001), p. 399.

15 Ibid.

16 Mendelssohn, 'Us Festival '83', p. 8.

17 Ibid.

18 Charles P. Wallace, 'Van Halen and 500 Friends', *Los Angeles Times* (31 May 1983).

19 Roth, *Crazy from the Heat*, pp. 260–61.

20 Ibid.

21 Quoted in Wozniak, *iWoz*, p. 256.
22 Mentioned in her review of the following year's show at the LA Forum [19 June 1981], *Sounds* (4 July 1981).
23 Canyon, 'Metal Daze'.
24 Rosen, 'Eddie Van Halen drops the bomb on Heavy Metal'.
25 Ibid.
26 Fredric Jameson, 'Periodizing the 60s', in *The Ideologies of Theory: Essays, 1971–86*, vol. II (Minneapolis, MN, 1988), pp. 204–8.
27 Robert Pattison, *The Triumph of Vulgarity: Rock Music in the Mirror of Romanticism* (Oxford, 1987), p. 176.
28 Mick Brown, 'The Secret of Van Halen's Excess', *Sunday Times Magazine* (20 January 1985).
29 Debby Miller, 'Van Halen's Split Personality', *Rolling Stone*, 424 (June 1984), p. 28.
30 Charles Dempsey, *Inventing the Renaissance Putto* (Chapel Hill, NC, 2001), quotation from front cover flap.
31 Dempsey, *Inventing the Renaissance Putto*, p. 63.
32 Steve Rosen, *Rock Talk, Vol. 1, Issue 1: Eddie Van Halen and David Lee Roth*, 1980 (digital audio music magazine) (Stoneworks, CA, 2007).
33 Steve Rosen, 'The Life and Times of Van Halen', in *Guitar World Presents Van Halen*, ed. Jeff Kitts, Brad Tolinski and Harold Steinblatt (Milwaukee, WI, 1997), p. 25.
34 Ibid., p. 53.
35 Steve Sutherland, 'The Gripes of Roth', *Melody Maker* (14 April 1984).
36 Ibid.

9 SAIL TO THE MOON

1 Matt Resnicoff, 'Jamming With Edward: Steve Morse, Albert Lee and the Emperor Van Halen', *Musician*, 151 (May 1991), p. 61.
2 Ibid, pp. 52–3
3 Timothy White, *The Nearest Faraway Place: Brian Wilson, The Beach Boys and the Southern California Experience* (London, 1996), p. 259.
4 See discussion in Robert Pattison, *The Triumph of Vulgarity: Rock Music in the Mirror of Romanticism* (Oxford, 1987), pp. 87–110.
5 Jeremy Strick, 'Visual Music', in *Visual Music*, ed. Kerry Brougher et al. (London, 2005), p. 15.
6 Douglas Kahn, *Noise, Water, Meat: A History of Sound in the Arts* (Cambridge, MA, 2001), p. 118.

7 Strick, 'Visual Music', p. 15.

8 John T. Hamilton, *Music, Madness and the Unmaking of Language* (New York, 2008), pp. 51–2.

9 Charles M. Young, 'The Oddest Couple: Can It Last', *Musician*, 68 (June 1984), p. 56.

10 Ibid.

11 Debby Miller, 'Van Halen's Split Personality', *Rolling Stone*, 424 (June 1984), p. 28.

12 John Livzey, 'Ed, Eddie, Edward', in *Guitar World Presents Van Halen*, ed. Jeff Kitts, Brad Tolinski and Harold Steinblatt (Milwaukee, WI, 1997), p. 87.

13 Barney Hoskyns, 'I Was a Teenage Gristleburger', *New Musical Express* (25 August 1984), p. 45.

14 Reyner Banham, *Los Angeles: The Architecture of Four Ecologies* (London, 1971), p. 221.

15 Ibid., p. 221.

16 Jas Obrecht, 'The Van Halen Tapes', in *Van Halen: Best of Guitar Player* (San Francisco, CA, 1993), p. 15.

17 Tom Beaujour and Greg Di Bennedetto, 'Cut and Dry', in *Guitar World Presents Van Halen*, p. 150.

18 Obrecht, 'The Van Halen Tapes', pp. 13–14.

19 Miller, 'Van Halen's Split Personality', p. 28.

20 Young, 'The Oddest Couple', p. 56.

21 Steve Sutherland, 'The Gripes of Roth', *Melody Maker* (14 April 1984).

22 Ibid.

23 Kahn, *Noise, Water, Meat*, p. 116.

24 Mattis, 'Scriabin to Gershwin', in *Visual Music*, ed. Brougher et al., p. 211.

25 Ibid.

26 Joe Bosso, 'The Monster of Rock: Eddie Talks about His Craft', in *Guitar World Presents Van Halen*, p. 111.

27 Obrecht, 'The Van Halen Tapes', p. 25.

28 David Wild, 'Balancing Act: Eddie Van Halen, the Rolling Stone Interview', *Rolling Stone*, 705 (April 1995), p. 44.

29 Geoff Dyer, *But Beautiful: A Book about Jazz*, 2nd edn (London, 1996), p. 195.

30 Howard Stern interview with Eddie Van Halen, SIRIUS radio (2006).

31 Eric Clapton, *Clapton: The Autobiography* (New York, 2007), p. 134.

32 Sutherland, 'The Gripes of Roth'.

33 Ibid.

34 Wild, 'Balancing Act', p. 44.

35 Jas Obrecht and Robert L. Doerschuk, 'The Buddy System', in *Van Halen: Best of Guitar Player*, p. 90.

36 Livzey, 'Ed, Eddie, Edward', in *Guitar World Presents Van Halen*, p. 91.

10 WIPEOUT, *C.* 1984–2007

1 W. T. Lhamon Jr, *Deliberate Speed: The Origins of a Cultural Style in the American 1950s* (New York, 1990), pp. 8–9.

2 Charles M. Young, 'The Oddest Couple: Can It Last', *Musician*, 68 (June 1984), p. 48.

3 David Lee Roth, *Crazy from the Heat* (New York, 2007), p. 233.

4 Ibid., p. 233.

5 James Halbert, 'The Gripes of Roth', *Classic Rock* (March 2004).

6 Frank Meyer, 'Eruption: The David Lee Roth Interview', *Popsmear*, 17 (September/October 1998).

7 Young, 'The Oddest Couple', p. 52.

8 Anthony Haden-Guest, 'Jewel of a Nile: Mr Rodgers Creates the Sound of the Eighties', *New York* (24 February 1986), p. 46.

9 Young, 'The Oddest Couple', p. 48.

10 David Fricke, 'Can This Be Love?', *Rolling Stone*, 477 (3 July 1986), p. 30.

11 David Wild, 'Balancing Act: Eddie Van Halen, the Rolling Stone Interview', *Rolling Stone*, 705 (April 1995), p. 49.

12 David Konow, *Bang Your Head: The Rise and Fall of Heavy Metal* (New York, 2002), p. 369.

13 Meyer, 'Eruption'.

14 'Laura Canyon' column, *Sounds* (11 June 1983).

DISCOGRAPHY AND SOUNDTRACK

VAN HALEN DISCOGRAPHY, 1978–83

Van Halen (Warner Bros K56470, February 1978)
Van Halen II (Warner Bros K56616, March 1979)
Women and Children First (Warner Bros K56793, March 1980)
Fair Warning (Warner Bros K56899, April 1981)
Diver Down (Warner Bros K57003, April 1982)
MCMLXXXIV/1984 (Warner Bros 92-3985, December 1983)

SOUNDTRACK

'And the Cradle Will Rock . . .' – Van Halen (1980)
'Moonlight Drive' – The Doors (1967)
'Could This Be Magic?' – Van Halen (1980)
'Light Up the Sky' – Van Halen (1979)
'Sick Again' – Led Zeppelin (1975)
'King of the Night Time World' – The Hollywood Stars (1974)
'Pipeline' – The Chantays (1963)
'Loss of Control' – Van Halen (1980)
'25 Hours a Day' – Jukebox Jimmy (Kim Fowley) (1974)
'Get Down Tonight' – KC and the Sunshine Band (1975)
'You're No Good' – Van Halen (1978)
'Strange Brew' – Cream (1967)
'Romeo Delight' – Van Halen (1980)
'I'm the One' – Van Halen (1978)
'Witchi Tai To' – Harpers Bizarre (1968)
'So This Is Love?' – Van Halen (1981)
'Dance With Your Baby' – Top Jimmy and the Rhythm Pigs (1987)
'Top Jimmy' – Van Halen (1983)
'Drop Dead Legs' – Van Halen (1983)

PHOTO ACKNOWLEDGEMENTS

The author and the publishers wish to express their thanks to the below sources of illustrative material and / or permission to reproduce it:

Author's collection: pp. 51, 66, 80, 81, 123, 146, 147, 181; Cache Agency: pp.4 2, 45, 47, 61 (© Jenny Lens); Corbis: pp.10 (Neal Preston), 25 (Bettmann), 77 (Lynn Goldsmith), 97 (Gary Leonard), 119 (Neal Preston), 141 (Roger Ressmeyer), 170 (Neal Preston), 184–5 (Mario Anzuoni / Reuters); Getty Images: pp. 31, 73, 103, 165, 173, 174.

INDEX

'1984' (song, Van Halen)
1984 (album, Van Halen)
 see *MCMLXXXIV*/1984
5150 studio 131, 132, 150, 154, 183, 186

Aesthetics of Rock (Meltzer) 108, 109, 114
'Ain't Talkin' 'Bout Love' (song, Van
 Halen) 73, 77, 96
'Alley Oop' (song, Hollywood Argyles)
 44
Amadeus (film) 178
Anaheim Stadium 7
Anthony, Michael 38, 63, 65, 67, 68, 96,
 143, 188
Astral Weeks (album, Van Morrison) 82
Avila, Eric 23

B-52s, The (band) 179
'Ballad of a Thin Man' (song, Bob Dylan)
 115
Banham, Reyner 87, 112, 113, 120, 161
Barrett, Syd 166
Baudelaire, Charles 157
Beach Boys, The 22, 106, 132, 155, 179
Beatles, The 21, 36, 83
Beat poets / writers 19, 107
Beck (singer) 183, 186
Belushi, John 91
Bennett, Tony 183

Berle, Marshall 47
Bertinelli, Valerie 176
Besant, Annie 52
'Beautiful Girls' (song, Van Halen) 180
'Big Bad Bill (Is Sweet William Now)
 128
Big Wednesday (film) 79
Bingenheimer, Rodney 32, 33, 41, 43, 44,
 46, 68
Binkley, Sam 27
Black Flag 88
Black Uhuru 122
Blackmore, Ritchie 28, 31
Black Sabbath 31, 56
Blake, William 145
Blasters, The 90, 96
Braga, Sonia 142
Bonham, John 28
Botnick, Bruce 74, 75
Bowie, David 30, 33, 138
'Break on Through (to the Other Side)'
 (song, The Doors) 75
Browne, Jackson 30
Brown, Mick 114, 148
'brown' sound / feel 8, 155–72
Budgie (band) 63
Buffalo Springfield, The 22, 23
Butterfield Blues Band 95
Byrds, The 22

Café Wha? 101, 102, *103*, 104, 106
Cage, John 176
California (see also Southern California)
   and esoteric spirituality 156
   hot rod culture 161
   as state of mind 49–50, 54, 55, 64
   as Promised Land 49–50, 54
   'sunshine state' 49
California Jam (festival, 1973) 31
Camarata, Salvador 'Tutti' 70
Campbell, Joseph 12
'Can't Find my Way Home' (song, Blind
   Faith) 124
Captain Beefheart 30, 78
Cathay de Grande (club) 94, 96, *97*, 98
Cervenka, Exene 91
Chic (band) 181
Chenier, Clifton 122
Chunky, Novi and Ernie 81
Church, Bill 83
Circle Jerks 88
Clapton, Eric 60, 124, 160, 169
Clash, The 90, 136, 138–40, 143, 188
Cochran, Eddie 22
'Cold Sweat' (song, James Brown) 37
Coltrane, John 161
Cooder, Ry 130, 132
Cooper, Alice 20, 26
Cope, Julian 166
Corso, Gregory 102
'Could This Be Magic?' (song, Van
   Halen)
Crazy From the Heat (David Lee Roth) 178,
   180, 181
Cream (band) 56, 159, 160
Creem (magazine) 18
'Crossroads' (song, Cream) 60
Crowley, Aleister 52

'Dance The Night Away' (song, Cream)
   159
'Dancing in the Street' (song, Van Halen)
   129
Dave Clark Five 59
Davis, Mike 53
Decline of Western Civilization (movie) 89
Deep Purple 63
Dempsey, Charles 149
Densmore, John 75
Derek and the Dominos 60
'Devil Gate Drive' (song, Suzi Quatro)
   35
DiMartino, Dave 18, 122
Disraeli Gears (album, Cream) 160
Diver Down (album, Van Halen) 15, 85, 86,
   120, 121, 127, 133
DOA (band) 96
Dogs, The (band) 47
Doobie Brothers 78
Doors, The 22, 25, 29, 31, 34, 74, 75, 91
'Do You Love Me' (song, Kiss) 70
Dyer, Geoff 169
Dylan, Bob 17, 36, 102, 103, 104, 105, 115

Eagles 31, 35
Electric Ladyland (studio) 46
Emerson, Lake and Palmer (ELP) 31
English Disco (Rodney Bingenheimer)
   32, 33, 34, 36
'Eruption' (song, Van Halen) 71, 72, 73

Fall, The (band) 121
Fair Warning (album, 1981) 16, 86, 96, 127,
   128
Farren, Mick 89
Flanner, Hildegarde 67
Fleetwood Mac 78
'Fopp' (song, Ohio Players) 37

'For What It's Worth' (song, Buffalo Springfield) 23
Fowley, Kim 33, 35, 41, 43, 46, 68, 70

Gazzarri, Bill 25, 29
Gazzarri's (club) 25, 28, 29, 30, 31, 32, 37
Geffen, David 41, 130
Gehman, Pleasant 93
Gehry, Frank 162
George, Lowell 85
Ginsberg, Alan 102
'Girl Gone Bad' (song, Van Halen) 18, 159, 160
Glam Rock (1970s) 33, 35, 44
'Go Away Little Girl' (song, Donny Osmond) 124
'God Bless the Child' (song, Billie Holiday) 145
Golden West Ballroom (Norwalk, CA) 94
Goodman, Mark (MTV) 141
'Good Vibrations' (song, The Beach Boys) 156
Gore, Tipper 13
Gray, Marcus 139, 140
Greenwich Village 101, 103, 105
Grétry, André
Guitarlos, Carlos 95
Guns n' Roses 25, 39

Hagar, Sammy 83, 180, 181, 188
Harpers Bizarre 78, 126
Harpers Bizarre 4 (album) 80
Havens, Richie 103, 104, 105, 106
Hawkins, Coleman 169
Heaven's Gate (cult) 52
Hendrix, Jimi 71, 102, 103, 170
Hoffmann, E.T.A. 155
Hollywood Argyles 44
Hollywood Hills 24

Hollywood music scene, early 1980s 87
Hollywood 'rock royalty' 28
Hollywood sign 26, 35
Holmes, Chris (WASP) 48
Hoskyns, Barney 18, 21, 32, 33, 39, 40, 41, 47, 161
Hostler, Larry 152
'Hot For Teacher' (song, Van Halen) 106, 158, 180
'House of Pain' (song, Van Halen) 159
Howdy Doody (1950s TV show) 15
Hurt, Mississippi John 122
Hyde, Lewis (Trickster Makes This World) 12, 18

Ice House (Pasadena club) 36
'I Feel Love' (song, Donna Summer) 129
'I'm So Glad' (song, Cream) 60, 160
'I'm the One' (song, Van Halen) 125, 126
'Indos' (Dutch Indonesians) 57, 58
'It's Your Thing' (song, Isley Brothers) 37

'Jamie's Cryin' (song, Van Halen) 124
James Gang (band) 38
Jameson, Fredric 144
Jett, Joan 35
John, Elton 30
'Johnny B. Goode' (song, Chuck Berry) 56, 98
Johnson, Robert 170
Jones, Mick (The Clash) 140
Jones, Steve (Sex Pistols) 76
Jukebox, Jimmy (aka Kim Fowley) 43, 44
Jullien, Francois 11
'Jump' (song, Van Halen) 145, 146, 149, 150, 158, 160
'Just A Gigolo' (song, David Lee Roth) 145, 147

KC and the Sunshine Band 38
Kelley, Pat 'Paraquat' 142
Kerouac, Jack 102, 105, 108, 109, 118, 133
Khan, Douglas 168
Kilgore, Terry 182
King, B. B. 169
'King of the Night Time World' (song, Kiss) 70
Kinks, The 38, 59, 128
Kiss (band) 46, 70
Krieger, Robby 75
KROQ (radio station) 44
Kubernik, Harvey 44

Ladanyi, Greg 30
Land of Sunshine (periodical) 50, 52
Landee, Donn 70, 71, 73, 76, 86, 131, 133, 134, 152, 176, 177
Lanza, Joseph 79
Layla and Other Assorted Love Songs 60
Laurel Canyon 24, 35, 41, 133–4
Led Zeppelin 22, 33, 126
Lennon, John 32, 34
Leonard, Gary 98
Lhamon, W. T. 69, 107
'Light My Fire' (song, The Doors) 75
Little Feat 78, 85
Live At Leeds (album, The Who) 63
Lopez, Trini 29, 38
Loud, Lance 47
Los Angeles Police Department (LAPD) 23, 89
Los Lobos 90, 96
Love (band) 22, 74
Lovin' Spoonful, The 179
Lummis, Charles 50

McWilliams, Carey 49, 52, 54, 126
Madonna 179
Mamas and the Papas, The 132
Manning, Peter 74
Manzarek, Ray 34, 35, 91
Marley, Bob 40
Masque, The (club) 90, 92
Mattis, Olivia 167
MCMLXXXIV/1984 (album, Van Halen) 17, 88, 131, 134, 144, 148, 175–8
'Mean Streets' (song, 1981) 16
Meat Loaf 30
Meltzer, Richard 108, 114
Mendelssohn, John 138, 139, 140
Messiaen, Olivier 167
Miller, Debby 158, 164
Minutemen, the 96
Mitchell, Joni 44
Monkees, The 33
Montrose (album, Montrose) 83, 124, 181
Montrose (band) 180
Montrose, Ronnie 83
Morrison, Van 30, 78, 82
Motels, The 47
Mötley Crüe 38, 100
Motown 122
Mott the Hoople 30
MTV 144
MTV Awards (1996) 183
Mullen, Brendan 90, 92, 93, 94
Mumps, The 45
'My Mother is a Space Cadet' (song, Dweezil Zappa) 133

Nicosia, Gerald 118
Nietzsche, Friedrich 108
Never Mind the Bollocks (album, the Sex Pistols) 76

Newman, Randy 130
New Musical Express (*NME*) 15
Nijmegen (Netherlands) 57
Nixon, Richard 26

'On Fire' (song, 1978) 8
One Flew Over the Cuckoo's Nest (film)
    158
On The Road (Kerouac) 109
On the Rox (bar) 32
Orbison, Roy 128
Ostin, Mo 144

Page, Jimmy 170
'Panama' (song, Van Halen) 18, 159
Paper Money (album, Montrose) 83
Parker, Charlie 68, 69, 73, 170
Parks, Van Dyke 130
Pasadena 48, *51*, 52, 53, 56, 83, 178
    and bohemianism 51
    and the Hanky
        Hacienda 62, 65
    and Mediterranean
        climate of 51, 52
Pasadena City College 124
Pasadena Civic Auditorium 60, 65
Patterson, Phast Phreddie 29, 98
Pattinson, Robert 109, 145
Peterson, John 80
Petty, Tom 47
Phonograph Record (magazine) 44, 46
Pigus Drunkus Maximus (album, Top
        Jimmy) 99
'Pipeline' (song, The Chantays) 59
Plant, Robert 44
Plimsouls, The 98, 99
Plugz, The (band) 88
Pochna, John 92, 93, 99

Polan, Dana 49–50
Pop, The (band) 47
Pop Art 19
Pop, Iggy 33, 34, 35
Presley, Elvis 34, 64
Prima, Louis 179
Prince 180
Priore, Domenic 21, 23
punk (1970s) 40, 41, 77
putti (Italian Renaissance) 146, 148, 149

Queen, Dave 121
Quiet Riot 135, 136

Rainbow Bar and Grill, the 28
Raitt, Bonnie 85
Ramones, The 94
Red Ball Jets (Roth band) 56, 182
Regan, Ron Jr 105
Repo Man (film) 87, 88
Rhodes, Bernie 139
Richards, Keith 40
Riot on Sunset Strip (film) 24
Rivers, Johnny 29, 38
Robinson, Lisa 60
Rock and Roll Hall of Fame 187, 188
Rodgers, Nile 179, 181, 182
Rolling Stones 22, 96, 124
Rollins, Henry 14
Romanticism 8, 156, 157, 166
'Romeo Delight' (song, Van Halen) 60
Rondstadt, Linda 35
Rose, Cynthia 15, 16, 17, 18
Rosen, Steven 115, 130, 143, 150
Roth, David Lee 42, 47, 52, 88, 113, 123, 141,
    174, *184–5*
    childhood 101–107
    and The Clash 138–140

work as Emergency Medical
  Technician 187
performance aesthetics 11–20, 36–7, 63,
  83, 84, 112, 116, 118, 119, 146
critical perception of 14–16
on heavy metal 135
post-Van Halen career, 180–87
life in Hollywood, early 1980s 87–100
outdoor adventuring 13
as trickster 12–14
Roth, Manny 101, 103, 104, 106
Roxy, The (club) 27, 29, 32, 40
'Runnin' with the Devil' (song, Van
  Halen) 67

Satori 112
Schoenberg, Arnold 167
Scriabin, Alexander 167
Sex Pistols 188
'Should I Stay or Should I Go' (song,
  The Clash) 139
Simmons, Gene 46
Simmons, Sylvie 142
skateboarding 64
Smiley Smile (album, The Beach Boys) 121
Snotty Scotty and the Hankies 62, 65, 67
Sonny and Cher 32
Snowden, Don 95
Sonics, The 95
Southern California
  attitude 18, 56, 112
  climate 53, 54, 64
  culture 8, 23, 24, 29, 64
Spector, Phil 22, 44, 132
Springsteen, Bruce 36, 78
Standells, The 24
Stanley, Paul 46
Stanton, Harry Dean 87

Starr, Kevin 7, 20, 50
Starr, Ringo 40
Starwood (club) 46, 68
Stern, Howard 183, 186, 188
Stone, Mark 62
'Strange Brew' (song, Cream) 60, 160
Strick, Jeremy 156
Strummer, Joe 138, 140
Sugerman, Danny 29, 32, 34
Sunset Marquis (hotel) 92
Sunset Sound Recorders (studio) 22, 67,
  70, 74, 75, 131
Sunset Strip 21–4, 25, 26–48, 65, 70, 72, 77
'Surf City' (song, Jan and Dean) 54
surfing 113, 175
Sutherland, Steve 166, 171
Suzuki, Daisetz 20, 110, 117, 149
Sweet, The 33
Swing You Sinners! (Max Fleisher cartoon)
  13
'Swing Sinners Swing!' (song, Van
  Halen) 16, 60
synaesthesia 156, 157
synthesized sound 74

Tatum, Art 68
teen culture (Los Angeles) 21
Templeman, Ted 68, 69, 70, 71, 72, 73, 76,
  77, 78, 79, 80, 81, 82, 83, 84, 85, 124,
  126, 128, 130, 131, 132, 152, 176, 177, 180
Temptations, The 121
Tewksbury, Drew 22
Tidwell, Sherriff Floyd 143
tone colour (music theory) 167, 168
Top Jimmy (aka James Koneck) 91, 94, 95,
  96, 97, 99
'Top Jimmy' (song, 1983) 18, 60, 88, 97, 98
'Top Ten Fruitcakes' (Melody Maker) 166

Townshend, Peter 112, 159, 170
Trashmen, The 108
T. Rex 33
Troubadour, The (club) 27, 29, 32, 100
Tupelo Honey (album, Van Morrison) 82
'Twist and Shout' (song) 38
Tytell, John 107, 116

'Unchained' (song, 1981) 16
unconscious, the, and
    creativity 8, 155–72
United Western Studios 131, 132
Us Festival 134–45

Vai, Steve 133
Valens, Richie 22
Valentine, Elmer 26
Van Halen
    band origins 56, 65
    cover songs 130
    performance 11
    songwriting process 150, 151, 152
    split with Roth 175–82
    and The Whisky A Go Go 45, 47, 61, 72
Van Halen (album) 66, 67, 74, 75, 76, 125,
    163, 167
    recording sessions 69, 71, 78
Van Halen II (album) 15, 84, 85
Van Halen, Alex 28, 131
    Dutch origins 55, 57, 58, 59
    response to critics 18
    drumming style 16
    'Eruption' 71, 72
Van Halen, Edward 21, 28, 73, 76, 123, 133–
    4, 154, 165, 170, 173, 174, 184–5
    'airiness' in guitar sound 73–4
    and creative process 155–72
    'Crossroads' (song) 60

'cures' cancer 186
Dutch origins 55, 57, 58, 59
'Eruption' 71, 72, 73
'Frankenstrat' guitar 161, 162, 164, 165,
    167
    guitar style 98, 159, 160, 162, 163
    and Hollywood club days 37, 38, 48, 61
    and spontaneity 77
    and Surf guitar 59, 60
Van Halen, Jan 59
Van Ronk, Dave 102
Vaughan, Stevie Ray
Velvet Underground 81
Venice Beach 23, 64, 77
Venus and the Razorblades 48
Vietnam War 24, 26
Village Recorders (studio) 22
Vinyl, Kosmo 138

Wainwright, Rufus 126
Waits, Tom 94
'Walk Don't Run' (song, The Surfaris) 59
Walker, Michael 27
Waller, Don 17, 88, 99
Walser, Robert 73
Warner Bros Records 48, 66, 78, 79, 80,
    81, 130
Watergate scandal 144
Waters, Muddy 122
Watts, Alan 101, 110
Webb School or
    California 105, 106
Western Recorders (studio) 22
Whisky A Go Go, The 26, 29, 34, 36, 42,
    45, 47, 48, 61, 68, 72, 88, 96, 100, 127
Who, The 112, 140, 159
Wickham, Andy 81
Wilson, Brian 86, 155, 156, 166

Winter, Edgar 179
'Witchi Tai To' (song, Harpers Bizarre)
    80
Wolf, Howlin' 122
Women and Children First (album, Van
    Halen) 85, 91, 92
Woodstock (film) 63, 104
Wolfe, Tom 27
Wozniak, Steve 137, 138, 142

X (band) 90

'Young and Wild' (song, Van Halen) 43,
    70
Young, Charles M. 11, 12, 16, 151, 158, 166,
    182
Young, Lester 169
Young, Neil 44
Your Filthy Little Mouth (album, David
    Lee Roth) 182

Zappa, Dweezil 133, 134
Zappa, Frank 73, 132, 133
Zen
    and Beat aesthetics 19, 110
    and childlikeness 8, 20, 149, 178
    and David Lee Roth 11, 14, 115, 155
    no-mind 111, 117, 188
    and transience 109
Zen California 8, 20, 152, 153
Zero One gallery 99
Zero-Zero (club) 91, 92, 93, 99
Zevon, Warren 30
Zlozower, Neil 134–5